PAUL STURMAN
Professor of harmony and composition
at the London College of Music
(formerly lecturer in music at
All Saints College of Education)

Creating music

LONGMAN

Introduction

What's the Score?

You must have asked people this question many times. The answer could be 15 all, 260 for 5, 2-0, and so on. But what else does 'score' mean? The dictionary says that score means 'to mark or cut with notches or lines', and 'a complete copy of a piece of music'.

If you were making something in wood and needed a guide line, you would score out this line by cutting a small groove in the wood. Score in music once meant much the same thing. A composer has always needed to write down all the parts for each player together. In this way he can see if the music fits, and what the overall sound will be like. In the 16th century, music manuscript paper was very expensive and difficult to get hold of. So the composer cut or scored his set of musical parts onto a wax tablet. When he had checked these over and was satisfied that they all fitted together, he copied out the separate parts for the performers. Then all he had to do was scrape off the top layer of wax and use the tablet again. This is why a complete copy of all the music for a piece is called a score.

A conductor needs a copy of the score. By looking at the score he will know when to start and stop the music in a tidy way by giving signals to the players. He will also know which instruments are playing at any given time, and can bring them in at the right moment.

How scores have changed
You will probably imagine a music score as looking something like this:

But it has taken composers thousands of years to learn how to write music in this way.

In the 6th century music was written down by using dashes, curves, hooks and dots:

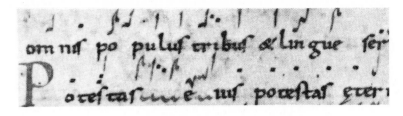

Byzantine music in the 11th century looked like this:

In the 12th century musicians used square notes and wrote them on four lines:

Music has also been written down in particular ways for different instruments. The lute (a guitar-like instrument) was as common in the 15th, 16th and 17th centuries as the piano is today. Lute music had letters or numbers instead of notes. The six lines are the six strings of the lute. The letters or numbers show the fret (or finger position) of each note to be played.

From the 15th to the 17th century, square and lozenge-shaped notes were used. These had stems and were written on five lines, called a stave or staff:

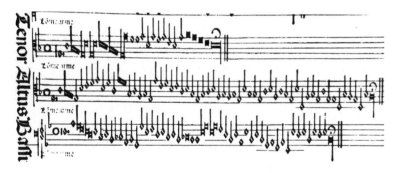

From this it was a short step to our present system of writing down music:

Composers today are still looking for new ways of writing down music. A modern computer score looks something like this:

3275 3751 3877 3962 2962 2438

2638 0343 0643 3988 2051 3051

The scores you are going to use in this book show 'sound-pictures'. Modern composers use these pictures as a kind of framework for the music, but the performers are often left to use their own ideas within this framework.

This picture of a score looks like what it is – a storm at sea. You can see the waves, spray, wind, rain and clouds. Each of the shapes tells the players when to play, for how long, and the dynamics (louds or softs) they are to use.

Notation

You will all have seen this kind of notation. It is the way we write down musical ideas.

From this short piece of music you can tell:

1. **The pitch of the notes** – how high or low the musical sounds are.
2. **The rhythm of the music** – the beat, how long each note is, and which notes are to be played with an accent (more strongly).
3. **The tempo** – the speed of the music. *Moderato* is an Italian word meaning to play or sing at a moderate speed.
4. **The dynamics** – how loud or soft the music is. *p* is short for *piano* (this is an Italian word for soft). *Crescendo* means get louder, and *diminuendo*, get softer.

About this book

There are nine projects in this book, and each one follows a similar plan. To start, you will find some interesting facts about the subject and some things to do. After this there is some music to play with hints on how to understand the score and play the music. The scores may look a bit odd at first, but they are really just 'sound-pictures'. This section may take several lessons to complete, especially if you are going to record the piece.

Then you will discover the sort of music that other composers have written on these subjects. This may be a piece written hundreds of years ago, or music from an up-to-date film such as *Jaws*.

Most people like to use their voices, and singing is second only to talking. There are all sorts of songs – rounds and canons, jazz, pop and comical – for you to sing. Some of these have piano accompaniment, but more often there are simple guitar chords and parts for percussion instruments, with a few strange noises as well! If you can't play the guitar, don't worry – the chords are quite easy to pick up with a little practice.

By this time you will know quite a lot about the subject. You will probably want to try out some of your own ideas, and experiment with different sounds. Some people are not as good at this as others, so there are a few ideas to use if you get stuck. At the end of each project there are quizzes, crosswords, and word puzzles.

Invent your own score

Draw out a plan like this on a large sheet of paper:

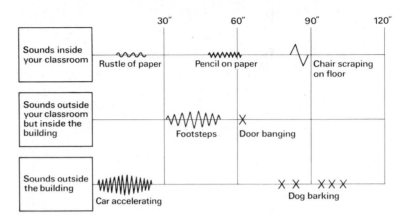

The idea of this activity is to make a score of the sounds around you. Be very quiet and listen to any sounds or noises around you for two minutes. You may hear some of the sounds on the plan, but listen for others and plot them down.

Also show on your score whether the sounds are high, low, loud, soft, short or long.

One person in the class should give a sign (a down-beat is best), to show the start of each 30-second section. When you have filled in these details, you will have your own score for this 'sound-picture'. This is how modern notation works.

When you have compared notes with your friends, make a performance of your score. You can imitate the sounds with your voices and instruments, or by using things around you. For example, tap a ruler or book on the desk for footsteps. Pay careful attention to the dynamics.

SPACE

The Moon, the Sun, the Stars,
Venus, Saturn, Mars,
Other planets . . .
I like space
Probed by Galileo
Journeyed by Apollo

The Sun
Bringing masses of Hydrogen
Masses of Helium
Millions of degrees
In the centre

And then . . .
The Planets
Pluto Cold,
Earth Old
Jupiter large
Mercury small
All different kinds
I like space.

– by an 11-year-old boy

The planet Earth seems very large to us but it is just a speck in the Universe. Earth is part of the Solar System which consists of planets, moons, asteroids, comets, meteorites, dust and gas, all revolving around the Sun. The Solar System is a very small part of our Galaxy. At least 400 million other galaxies can be detected from Earth.

The stars are so far away that scientists measure their distances in light years. (A light year is six million, million miles – 6,000,000,000,000.)

The brightest star in our sky is called Sirius. It is one of the nearest stars to Earth, but its light takes more than eight years to travel to Earth. Some stars are so far away that it takes hundreds of years for their light to reach us.

If you look at the sky on a clear night it may appear at first glance to be a confusing mass of stars. But it does not take long to spot groups of stars and planets. There are certain groups of stars which, if you can recognise them, you can use as 'landmarks' to help you to find other stars.

Things to do

1. Copy this drawing of star shapes onto a piece of card. Look at the shape of the Plough. (This is part of the Great Bear.) It is made up of seven bright stars. Follow the last two stars of the Plough – called pointers – to find the Pole Star.

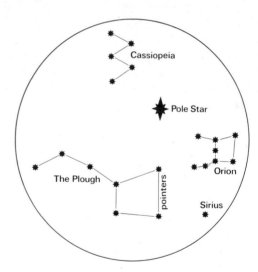

2. Take your star card outside with you on a dark, clear night. You will also need a dim torch, or you can cover a torch with red paper so that you can use it to look at the card. Look at the sky and try to identify some of the groups of stars, using your card to help you. The Plough will probably be the easiest one to find at first. Two other groups to look for are Cassiopeia and Orion. Cassiopeia is shaped like the letter W and Orion is sometimes said to look like a giant with three stars for his belt.

Journey through the galaxy

You are now going to play a piece of music about a journey through our Galaxy. This is in the shape of a spiral, rather like a watch-spring.

If you look at the score of music on the opposite page you will see that the Sun's heat is at the centre. This is where the music begins. On the journey around the spiral you pass gleaming planets, groups of asteroids and meteorites. You will also notice bright, sparkling groups of stars, and then some older stars. These are a deeper orange or red in colour. There are also clouds of dust and gas. Travelling on round the spiral, sometimes in silence except for the Sun's heat, you pass by a single star. This is brighter than any other star you have seen. The journey ends as you reach the edge of the Galaxy and the sounds die away.

Music for you to play
You will need a conductor and eight groups of players for this piece. The music starts at the middle of the score, and works round the spiral in an outward direction.

THE CONDUCTOR
Give a down-beat every 10 seconds (10″). (The Sun's rays shining through the Galaxy are the 10-second sections.)

GROUP 1 **The Sun**
This sound lasts for the whole piece. It should get gradually louder, then softer, then louder again, throughout the piece.

A good instrument to use for this is an electronic organ. If you are lucky enough to have an organ at school, play the group (or cluster) of notes which you see inside the Sun sign on the score. Hold these notes down right through the music. You can make the sound louder and softer by pushing the foot pedal (swell pedal) slowly up and down.

A piano would make a good alternative to the organ. If you are using a grand piano, prop up the lid. An upright piano will need to have the front taken off. Brush the high (shorter) strings with your fingers. Be sure to keep the right pedal of the piano held down. This will make the sounds last longer. Brush the strings again when the sounds die away.

You could also use tuning forks as well as, or instead of, a piano. Use as many players as you can get tuning forks, one for each player. You can play these by tapping one of the prongs on some hard rubber or soft wood, or you can pinch the two prongs together and let go smartly.

You may find it useful to record the sounds on a tape recorder. When you have made the recording, experiment by changing the playback speed. Decide if the sound is better at a fast, normal or slow speed. The recording will need to last for the whole piece ($3\frac{1}{2}$ minutes) whatever speed you decide to use. If you pick the fast speed, twice as much music will be needed as at the normal speed. It is better to have too much music rather than too little. You can always switch off after $3\frac{1}{2}$ minutes.

GROUP 2 **The planets**
Hit gongs or large cymbals with soft sticks and let the sounds die away naturally.

GROUP 3 **Star clusters**
Use different-sized triangles and chime bars for these stars. Play groups of notes with hard sticks and beaters.

GROUP 4 **Single, brighter stars**
Play single notes on glockenspiels with hard beaters. The sound should be quite loud and bright. Let the sound ring on.

GROUP 5 **Small groups of older stars**
Use the middle and low notes of the xylophone and hit the bars with hard sticks.

GROUP 1

GROUP 2

GROUP 3

GROUP 4

GROUP 5

GROUP 6

GROUP 7

GROUP 8

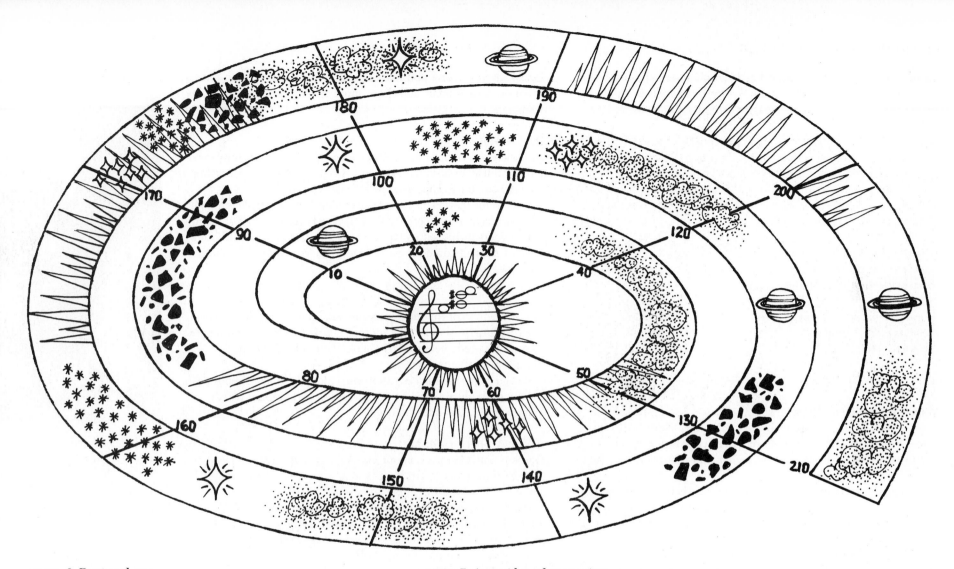

GROUP 6 Dust and gas

There are two groups of sounds here:

1. For the dust, use maracas and sandblocks. The maracas should be lightly shaken and slowly rolled around, and the sandblocks should be rubbed lightly together.

2. For the gas, use your voices to make sounds like *shhh* and *whoooosh*.

GROUP 7 Asteroids and meteorites

Use timpani and other drums, and hit them with soft and hard beaters. To make the sounds for the asteroids and meteorites whistling through space, play a slide whistle or recorder mouthpiece to make sliding sounds.

GROUP 8 The Sun's rays

Pour different amounts of water into some wine glasses. Dip your finger in the water, then rub it lightly and evenly round the rim of the glass. Before you play in the piece, practise doing this until you can make a continuous whistling sound.

Listening

Gustav Holst (1874–1934) was a British composer who was very interested in ancient legends and astrology. His interest in Space inspired him to write a suite (or group of pieces) for orchestra called *The Planets*.

In the past, people believed that the planets influenced their lives. Some people still believe this to be true. There are very many people who read their horoscopes each day.

Holst composed this suite of seven pieces and gave each piece the name of one of the planets. He wrote this music for a very large orchestra. The pieces are called:

Mars – the Bringer of War
Venus – the Bringer of Peace
Mercury – the Winged Messenger
Jupiter – the Bringer of Jollity
Saturn – the Bringer of Old Age
Uranus – the Magician
Neptune – the Mystic

'The character of each planet suggested lots to me.'

Mars – the Bringer of War
Holst shows us the character of this red, angry planet with its fierce dust storms. He uses loud blocks of chords and a pounding rhythm. These two ideas become louder and more fierce as the music moves on.

The music starts with an *ostinato* which is heard many times:

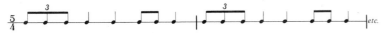

Ostinato is an Italian word, and it stands for a fragment of melody or a rhythm that is heard over and over again.

Near the middle of the piece the rhythm changes. The brass instruments blare out a new tune:

This music is rather like the early jazz (called Ragtime) that was popular at this time.

There is a huge climax as the organ joins in and the earlier tunes are heard again.

A lot of interesting and exciting music has been written for television programmes and films about space. Here are just a few examples:

Doctor Who

This science fiction serial has been on television for many years, and the music by Ron Grainer and the BBC electronic workshop is still very similar to that used in the first episodes.

The Doctor travels in a weird space ship that looks like a police box. He has met and dealt with Daleks, Cybermen, Wirrons and giant spiders in his job as President of the Time Lords. Although different music is used for each series, the title music stays much the same.

Star Trek

Star Trek is one of the most popular television series ever made. The USS Enterprise was sent on a five year mission to 'go where no man has gone before'. Mr. Spock is one of the popular characters in the programme.

Many composers have written music for the different episodes, but the main music used to introduce the programme was composed by Alexander Courage.

2001: A Space Odyssey

This is a film adventure about a voyage to outer space. You find yourself hurtling through giant star clusters, clouds of exploding gas, and even see whole new suns being born.

The main music used for 2001 was composed many years before the film was made by the German composer, Richard Strauss, in 1896. The music is called *Also Sprach Zarathustra*. This music is very exciting and most people will immediately recognise it without knowing its correct title!

Close Encounters of the Third Kind

This is a film about a meeting with beings from another planet. Their communication signal is five musical notes:

Play this signal on an instrument. You will almost certainly recognise it.

Doctor Who and K9 stand outside their time machine, the Tardis

Singing

There are many songs about space, but this one has been composed specially for you to sing. The words are rather a mixture – they come from the Bible (the Creation story) and a nursery rhyme and include the star sign names from your horoscope.

There are two accompaniments to this song, **A** and **B**. You can play the part for guitars, glockenspiels and xylophones (**A**), or one of you could play the piano part (**B**). You can use either **A** or **B**, or play both together to add to the fun.

Your own compositions

In *Mars* from *The Planets*, you will remember that Holst uses an *ostinato*.

If you listen to film music and the music of some television advertisements, you are almost sure to hear ostinatos being used. (Remember that an ostinato is a tune or rhythm that is played over and over again.)

For your own music, look at this picture which is about the arrival of beings from another planet. Use the five-note signal from the film *Close Encounters of the Third Kind* as an ostinato. This ostinato will provide a background or bass to the music you invent to go with the picture. Here are two ideas to try:

1. Make up some music to play with the ostinato.
2. Divide into two groups (humans and space creatures) and play the five-note signal to each other in different ways. (In *Close Encounters* the five notes are played in many different ways by the humans and space creatures as they try to make contact – slow or fast, high or low. Sometimes the five-note conversation overlaps so that the humans and the space creatures are playing at the same time.) By doing this you will be making a kind of space musical conversation.

The humans watch as the space creatures arrive

Space quiz

On your travels you may meet with hostile creatures, so this is your secret code for contacting Earth.

The Code:

Use the code to find the titles of these pop songs and films about space.

Songs

1. ⌒ ÷ ∧ ⊙ ⌄ △   ⊡ ⧄ ⊡
   by ⌄ ○ △ ÷ ⊡   ⊠ ÷ ⊤ ⊡

2. △ ⊳ ⧄ ∧ ⌄   ÷ △ △ ⊡ △ ⚲
   by △ ⧄ ◖ ⊡ △   □ ÷ ⊲ ⊡ ⌄

3. ⊡ ⊡ △ ⌄ ⌒ ⊳ ○ ⧄ ⊡ ⊡ ⌄ △ ⧄ ⌒ ⚲   ∧ ⌒ ⧄ ⌒ △
   by △ ⊤ ⌄   ∧ ⧄ ⌒ ⊳ ⌄ ⊡ △ ⌄ ⌒ △

Films

1. △ △ ⧄ ⌒   ⊲ ⧄ ⌒ △

2. □ ⧄ △ △ ○ ⌄ △ △ ⧄ ⌒   ÷ ⧄ ○ ⧄ ∧ △ ⊡ ∧ ⧄

3. ⊡ ÷ ÷ ⊡ ⌒ ⧄ ⊙ ⌄ ⌒

Now that you know how the code works, you and your friends could use it to send secret messages.

the sea

The seas and oceans cover nearly three quarters of the Earth's surface. Earth is the only planet in the Solar System with a large amount of water on its surface.

There are five oceans – Atlantic, Pacific, Indian, Arctic and Antarctic, as well as many seas, gulfs, bays and rivers. Altogether, this great body of water makes up one huge ocean of more than 300 million cubic miles.

A drop of water that splashes against a rocky coast in the Atlantic one day may touch a coral reef in the Pacific some months or years later.

You can learn a great deal about the sea by taking a walk along a beach. As you get closer to the beach you will notice the fresh smell of the sea and feel the cool breeze against your skin.

On a summer's day there will be people swimming, seagulls overhead and perhaps a fishing boat in the distance. On the beach you will find pebbles, shells and driftwood. When the tide goes out it leaves shells of many shapes and colours.

Near Studland in Dorset there are some 'musical sands'. If you walk on the sand there, or drag a stick over the surface, you will hear a high, 'singing' sound.

The Sea – by James Reeves

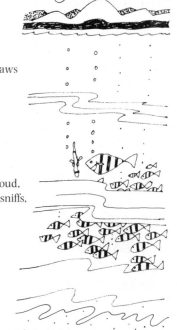

The sea is a hungry dog,
Giant and grey.
He rolls on the beach all day.
With his clashing teeth and shaggy jaws

Hour upon hour he gnaws
The rumbling, tumbling stones,
And 'Bones, bones, bones, bones!'
The giant sea-dog moans,
Licking his greasy paws.

And when the night wind roars
And the moon rocks in the stormy cloud,
He bounds to his feet and snuffs and sniffs,
Shaking his wet sides over the cliffs,
And howls and hollos long and loud.

But on quiet days in May or June,
When even the grasses on the dune
Play no more their reedy tune,
With his head between his paws
He lies on the sandy shores,
So quiet, so quiet, he scarcely snores.

Things to do

1. Make a collection of pebbles of many different shapes and sizes. Hit them together to make different sounds.
2. Collect small shells and use them to make a mobile. Make a small hole in each of the shells and hang them on pieces of strong thread. When they are moved they will make a tinkling sound.
3. Make your own musical sands. Get some bowls or jars and put different amounts of sand into them. Hit the bowls or jars with a stick. Each of them should make a different sound.
4. Explore rock pools on a beach. Find out all you can about the creatures you find there, such as crabs or starfish.
5. Visit a maritime museum such as the one at Greenwich, or go to have a look at a famous ship such as Discovery on the River Thames.

Storm at sea

The sea with its raging waves is one of the most destructive and terrifying forces in the world. Waves can shatter the strongest pier, or toss a house into the air and carry it away.

You are now going to play a piece of music about a violent storm at sea. For this piece it will help if you imagine large, rough waves pounding against the seashore with a loud roar. They roll and crash, the wind howls, the rain begins and the drops become heavier. In the music there are sounds of seafoam, mighty breakers, wind and rain, flying stones and sand, booming and terrifying sounds. All these things make a dramatic musical picture of a storm at sea.

Music for you to play

You will need a conductor and six groups of players to play the music. The music score is divided into 20-second sections, each marked by a vertical line. Follow the signs for your group on the score and watch for the conductor's down-beat. He will give a down-beat at the beginning of each section of the score, but this is only a guide to let you know how the time is going. It does not matter if you come in a little early or late, but it is important not to miss your entry altogether. When you have played the music several times and are happy with the result, make a tape-recording of the piece so that you can hear how your piece sounds.

THE CONDUCTOR
Give a down-beat every 20 seconds (20″).

GROUP 1 **Waves and breakers**
Play soft rolls on cymbals, gongs and drums. Use soft beaters, and make the sounds louder when the waves get higher on the score. Practise doing the roll until you can play the sounds quite quickly. (A good player can make the roll sound almost like one long note.)

GROUP 1

GROUP 2 **Spray and seafoam**
Use glockenspiels and small triangles. Play patterns of notes with hard beaters, but make them quick and short.

GROUP 2

GROUP 3 **Flying sand and stones**
Use three main instruments here: *maracas* shake these quite hard; *sandblocks* rub these together quickly; *carpet tacks in a drum skin* roll these around. You can also use the real thing if you have collected some pebbles and stones from the beach. Hit these together for the flying stone sounds.

GROUP 3

GROUP 4 **The wind**
Use your voices to make sounds like *hoow*, *shshew* and *heeeeew*. Blow across the top of an empty bottle and use recorder mouthpieces and whistles to make the sound of the wind. The wind starts in small gusts, then builds up to gale force. As the wind rises and falls, make the sounds louder and higher, then softer and lower.

GROUP 4

GROUP 5 **The rain**
Play quick repeated notes on several xylophones using hard beaters, and hit claves together.

GROUP 5

GROUP 6 **Clouds**
Draw your fingers or soft beaters across the piano strings. Keep the right pedal pressed down all through the piece. This will help to keep the notes sounding. As the clouds get blacker and larger, your sounds should become louder.

GROUP 6

'The sea has been very good to me. She has shown me all her moods.'

Listening

Claude Debussy (1862–1918), a French composer, loved the sea. He composed three pieces for a large orchestra and called these *La Mer* (French for 'The Sea').

He wrote to a friend in 1903:

'I was destined for the happy life of a sailor, but the hazards of existence led me in another direction. Nevertheless, I have always retained a sincere passion for Her (the sea). I have an endless store of memories about the sea.'

La Mer

FIRST MOVEMENT From Dawn to Noon at Sea

Different pictures of the sea are heard at different times of the day in this first piece. The music starts mysteriously and slowly as the first signs of daylight catch the sea. Debussy captures the rise and fall of the waves with music that grows and swells. After the sea awakes there is a huge climax. The music ends with a hymn-like tune played by the brass instruments. This is the sea under the midday sun.

SECOND MOVEMENT The Waves at Play

This playful piece is full of movement and uses three main tunes. The first tune is played by the cor anglais. The cor anglais (sometimes called an English horn) is a large kind of oboe which can play lower notes than the oboe. These two instruments sound very much alike, but the cor anglais looks rather different because of the bulge at the bell end.

The second tune is played by the violins and begins with two trills. (A trill is a shake between two different notes.)

oboe   cor anglais

The third tune is played by the solo horn.

If you copy out these tunes and join the notes together with a line, you will see that their shapes are very like the wave shapes.

THIRD MOVEMENT Dialogue between the Wind and the Sea

The music is more dramatic here as the sea gets more and more restless. There is an angry opening when the trumpet plays a tune heard in the first movement. The music surges and swells to a climax and the brass instruments end the music. They seem to whip the wind and sea to a furious and exciting finish.

Films about the sea

You must have seen some of the popular films about the sea: *Orca the Whale*, *The Deep*, *Jaws* and *Raise the Titanic*. (The Titanic was a ship which sank on its maiden voyage.) These all rely on music to help make the action exciting and dramatic.

Jaws, one of the most popular films ever, is a spine-chilling story of a man's fight against a giant killer shark that terrorizes a small holiday resort. John Williams composed the music for this film. He captures the scenes of danger and excitement very well. Quiet and mysterious music represents the fish moving silently through the water, but you immediately sense in the music that danger is present. The mood of the music changes as the shark thrashes its tail about and attacks. It has claimed another victim!

Picture from the poster advertising the film, 'Jaws'

Singing

Many sea-songs (called shanties) were sung to make work easier to do and less boring on ships. The man who started up the song was called the shantyman. He would sing a verse, and the sailors joined in with the chorus as they were working. The rhythm of the song helped to keep them together.

There are three types of shanty:

1. *Short haul* – these jobs had only a few pulls, such as hauling sheets, tacks and braces.

2. *Halyard* – these were longer and more exhausting jobs, such as hoisting the 'yards' (ropes joined to the sail).

3. *Capstan* – very long and slow jobs, for example, heaving in the anchor or manning the pumps.

Bound for the Rio Grande is a capstan shanty.

Bound for the Rio Grande

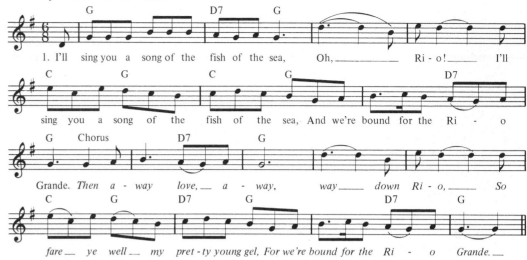

1. I'll sing you a song of the fish of the sea, Oh, _____ Ri - o! _____ I'll sing you a song of the fish of the sea, And we're bound for the Ri - o Grande. *Then a - way love, _____ a - way, way _____ down Ri - o, _____ So fare _____ ye well _____ my pret - ty young gel, For we're bound for the Ri - o Grande.* _____

2. Sing goodbye to Sally, and goodbye to Sue,
   Oh, Rio!
   And you who are listening, goodbye to you.
   And we're bound for the Rio Grande.
   Chorus

3. Our ship went sailing out over the Bar,
   Oh, Rio!
   And we pointed her nose for the Southern Star.
   And we're bound for the Rio Grande.
   Chorus

15

Your own compositions

Make up some tunes for these short poems. Use chime bars, glockenspiels or xylophones, and play any or all of these six notes. First, tap the rhythm of the words. Then invent your tune.

DOH — C   RAY — D   ME — E   SOH — G   LAH — A   DOH — C

The wave comes and goes,
Splashing over your toes,
You gasp to greet it
Shoulders bent to meet it.

The wind that blows,
The ship that goes,
Was not the sea
Made for the free.

At Greenwich lies the Cutty Sark,
A noble ship was she,
Around the world in pride she sailed
To carry a cargo of tea.

While the raging seas did roar,
And the stormy winds did blow,
We jolly sailor boys were up, up aloft,
And the landlubbers lying down below.

When you have invented your tunes, add some sound effects to the music. It is quite easy to make up sea sounds with instruments. Maracas, shakers, sandblocks, slither boxes, jingles and claves will all be useful. Use jingles and claves to add colour to your music and to suggest the sea washing onto the stones at the water's edge. Chime bars and glockenspiels are good for making sparkling water sounds. Experiment with more unusual sounds like those you tried out in the 'Things to do' section.

Sea quiz

This is a crossword puzzle built around the word sandcastle. Copy the puzzle framework out onto a piece of paper, or use a piece of tracing paper large enough to cover the puzzle, and use that to write your answers on.

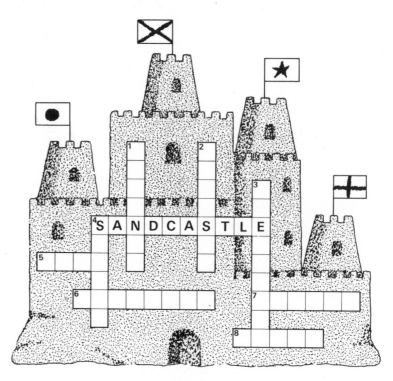

Clues down
1. The name of the famous ship which sank on its maiden voyage
2. This French composer wrote La Mer
3. The Cutty Sark is docked at . . . . .
4. Name for a sea song

Clues across
5. Film title – . . . . . the Whale
6. Where in Dorset are the musical sands?
7. Name of one of the five oceans
8. What kind of fish was Jaws?

WINTER

Snowing

On a Winter day
The flakes of snow
Fall like broken clouds
To the earth below

As I look up
I feel the flakes
As soft as wool
Brushing my face

The sky is a roof
That has fallen down
Scattering white pieces
Over the ground

Rabbits and birds
That live outdoors
Fluff up their fur
And ruffle their feathers

Though the roof has fallen
And it begins to freeze
They keep themselves warm
In their house in the fields.

by Stanley Cook

Winter is not such a colourful season as spring, summer or autumn, but it is not as lifeless as you might think.

The countryside is often quiet and empty at this time of year, but there are still some plants which have brightly-coloured berries and we know that there are many plants growing beneath the surface of the ground, waiting for the arrival of the spring.

Winter is the season of long, dark days, with ice, fog, snow and cold winds. But the season is brightened by Christmas with presents, decorations, holly and mistletoe to look forward to.

Snow is really ice shaped into very small crystals. When it is snowing you will often be able to catch a snowflake in your hands, or better still, on a piece of dark card or felt. Have a quick look at the snowflake under a magnifying glass before it melts. You will be amazed at what you see.

The detail of one snowflake is never the same as another, although they are all hexagonal (six-sided) in shape. These pictures are of different snowflake patterns:

Things to do

1. Make a collage on the winter theme. (A collage is a collection of pictures and objects put together in an interesting way and stuck down to make a picture.) Here are a few ideas that you can use but you will be able to think of others for yourself.

a) Draw some snowflake patterns on paper, or cut polystyrene tiles into snowflake shapes.

b) Collect leaf skeletons. (These are leaves which have rotted away to leave just the veins or skeleton shape of the leaf.) If you cannot find a leaf skeleton, use an ordinary leaf to make a print of the skeleton shape. This is how you do it: Put some leaves onto a piece of paper with their undersides facing upwards. Use a roller to coat each leaf with paint. Then press the painted sides of the leaves onto your collage. Use leaves of different shapes and sizes.

c) Make a tree bark rubbing. Put some paper over part of the bark of a tree. Rub a wax crayon over the paper. The pattern of the tree bark will show through on the paper.

2. Make some Christmas cards using snowflake patterns or leaf skeleton prints.

Wintry scene

Imagine a wintry scene just like those on Christmas cards and calendars. It is a clear, frosty evening. The village clock strikes six. The stars are sparkling brightly in the sky and their reflections shine in a frozen lake. All around are mountains, and warm, coloured lights blaze out from little cottage windows. There are hard, steep rocks along the edge of the frozen lake. The air is clear and cold. Against this quiet, wintry scene, we hear the excited, chattering voices of people skating on the ice.

Music for you to play

The piece you are going to play describes in music this clear and frosty evening. You will need a conductor and six groups of players for this piece. Groups 1, 2, 3 and 4 set the scene. Groups 5 and 6 are the skaters. Watch for the conductor's down-beat every 30 seconds. This will help you to find your way on the score.

THE CONDUCTOR
Give a down-beat every 30 seconds (30").

GROUP 1 The mountains
Play soft rolls on a gong and large, suspended cymbals, getting gradually louder and softer as your sign on the score gets larger and smaller. The sound should never be too loud as the mountains are in the distance.

Other people in this group can make sounds by gently running soft-headed drumsticks up and down over the lower (thicker) strings inside the piano. All the sounds should be allowed to ring on after you have played them.

GROUP 2 Lights blaze out from the cottage windows
Play this group of notes on glockenspiels. The sounds should be bright, so use hard or metal beaters. Let the sounds continue until they die away.

GROUP 3 The village clock and the steep rocks
The players in this group have two sounds to make. The village clock is heard only at the beginning of the music, so the same players will be able to change instruments and play for the steep rocks later in the piece. Hit tubular bells with a wooden mallet for the sound of the clock striking six. Make the sounds for the steep rocks by hitting metal rods together. Metal beaters will do, or you could carefully take chime bars off their stands and use them instead.

GROUP 4 Clear sparkling stars and their reflections in the ice
Use triangles to make all the sounds for the stars and their reflections. Hit the triangles with metal beaters. Use small (10cm or 4 inch) triangles for the stars and larger triangles for the reflections. Let the sounds ring on.

GROUP 5 The sounds of the skates on the ice
There are two different sounds for this group to play. Part of the group should use cymbals (any size will do) and play them by rubbing the surface lightly with either wire brushes or metal beaters. The rest of the group uses wine glasses with different amounts of water in them. Dip your finger into the water, then rub it round the rim of the glass lightly and evenly.

GROUP 6 Excited, chattering voices
Use your voices to make the sounds of the excited skaters. Think about skating on ice – the air feels sharp on your face and in your nose; your hands are cold and you blow on your fingers to keep them warm. As you take a sharp breath your teeth chatter a little but you are happy and excited. Rub your hands together and make clapping noises. Use your voices for sounds like *ooooh* (sucking the breath in) and *huuuh* (breathing out). While you pretend to skate around, talk to your friends:
'Isn't it cold?' 'Hey! Look at him.' 'Be careful.'

Think of other phrases you might use as well. Although your sounds will be heard right through the piece, be careful not to drown the other sounds by being too loud.

GROUP 1

GROUP 2

GROUP 3

GROUP 4

GROUP 5

GROUP 6

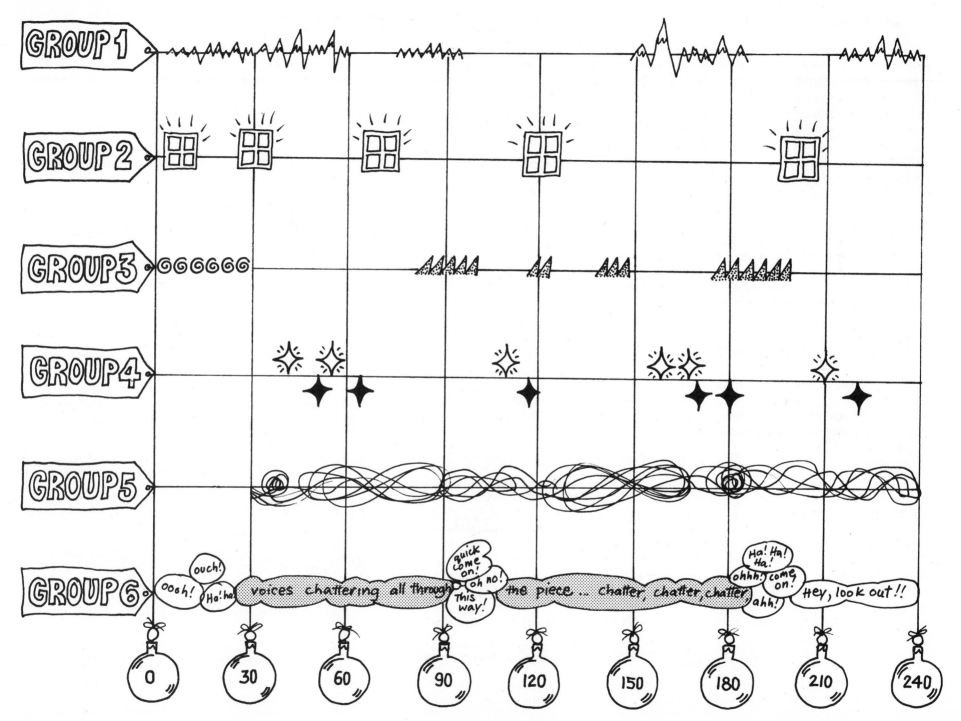

Listening

The Four Seasons by Vivaldi

Antonio Lucio Vivaldi was born in Venice in 1678, and died in Vienna in 1741. At the age of twenty-five he was ordained as a priest, but spent most of his time teaching the violin and composing because he was so interested in music. He wrote more than 40 operas and 400 concertos. He is often called the 'red-haired priest' because of the colour of his hair.

The Four Seasons is Vivaldi's most famous work. Each of the seasons; spring, summer, autumn and winter, is represented in a concerto in three movements for solo violin and string orchestra. *Concerto* is an Italian word, and concertos are usually pieces for one solo player and an orchestra (although many early concertos used several soloists).

In *The Four Seasons* there are descriptions of all kinds of weather, and there is a short phrase from a poem written above the music every now and then. This tells us what is happening in the music.

Listen to the concerto called *Winter* (L'Inverno). At the front of the score for this concerto, there is printed a twelve-line poem. Each line of the poem is given a letter (**A**, **B**, **C** and so on).

FIRST MOVEMENT (fast)

A The first line of the poem is about freezing and shivering in the cold. The strings play lots of repeated short notes, just as if they were trembling with cold.

B The solo violin then shows us 'the horrid winds'.

C This line of the poem is about 'stamping our feet to keep warm'.

The string instruments play *martellato*. This is an Italian word which means 'hammered'. In other words, the playing is to be in short, sharp strokes on the strings, and played with the very point of the bow.

D The next line of the poem speaks about our teeth chattering. Vivaldi has written some clever music here with the solo violin playing with double stopping. (This is when the soloist plays on two strings of the violin at the same time.) The other instruments play short, repeated notes, and you can just imagine the freezing cold, causing your teeth to chatter as you listen to the music.

SECOND MOVEMENT (slow)

This slow movement is a complete contrast to the exciting and descriptive music of the first movement. The music is about only one line of the poem.

E This line describes sitting by the fire-side, quiet and content, while the rain pours down on hundreds of other poor people outside. The soloist plays a 'singing' kind of tune, and the other strings accompany with smooth and flowing music.

THIRD MOVEMENT (fast)

The last seven lines of the poem are used in this final movement. First, we hear music for walking on solid ice (**F**).

Line **G** is about walking carefully in case of falling down.

H – here it happens! The words describe turning round quickly and falling over! Vivaldi writes music for this event that slides around with quick, falling runs of notes:

I – after the fall, the poet gets up on the ice again, but **L** – the ice breaks! There are four quick notes followed by a rest in the music. These are heard three times:

M A new section describes the wind, with music rising and falling. You can just imagine the wind blowing from listening to the music.

N The last line of the poem shows the north and south winds blowing hard with some very gusty music.

Singing

Here is a song about the weather for you to sing. It has some rather silly words. The chorus comes twice, and is a tongue-twister, with a pun on the word weather. (A pun is a word which sounds like another word, but has a different meaning.)

The words of the verse always seem to be contradicting themselves. Start by singing the chorus at a steady speed. Then, when you repeat the chorus (after the verse) try to sing the words at double the speed. The accompaniment is for the piano.

Your own compositions

The French composer, Debussy, wrote a descriptive piece for piano called *The snow is dancing*. When it is snowing, the flakes seem to be dancing as they fall to the earth. Debussy's music describes their movement well.

To make your own piece called 'The snow is dancing', imagine the shape of a snowflake which has been put onto a xylophone, glockenspiel or piano keyboard. It will look something like this:

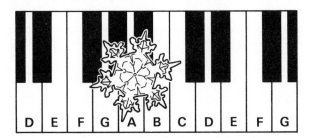

Play the notes which the six points of the snowflake touch. You can add variety to your music by playing these six notes in different rhythms, on different instruments, and by using the notes in a different order. Use some of the other snowflake patterns in the same way. Then play all the different snowflake pattern tunes together in your piece.

What you are really doing here is looking at the shape of something and then making music with similar shapes or patterns.

Another idea along these lines could be the shape of icicles. These have a jagged shape:

so think of music that goes sharply up and down, for example:

Invent some other shapes that could be used in the same way for your own music about winter.

Winter quiz

1. Pantomimes

Winter is the traditional time for pantomimes. The titles of these pantomimes are not correct. Sometimes they are just the opposite of what they should be. Give them their proper names.

a) Jetblack and the seven giants
b) Cat in slippers
c) John and the pea stick
d) Rockafella and the two good looking brothers
e) Father duck that laid the silver egg
f) Large blue walking hat

2. Christmas Crossword

COLOURS

The world is made beautiful by colour. The blue sky changes to red at sunset. Clouds are white and grey. Stars can be white, blue, yellow or red. Flowers come in many colours. Leaves change colour in autumn to yellow, red and brown, but the grass stays green. Your home has coloured walls and furniture. Clothes and food are also very colourful.

Some colours, like orange, red and yellow are warm colours. Green, grey, blue and purple can be rather cold colours.

Colours by Christina Rossetti

What is pink? a rose is pink
By the fountain's brink.
What is red? a poppy's red
In its barley bed.
What is blue? the sky is blue
Where the clouds float through.
What is white? a swan is white
sailing in the light.

What is yellow? pears are yellow,
Rich and ripe and mellow.
What is green? the grass is green
With small flowers between.
What is violet? clouds are violet
In the summer twilight.
What is orange? why, an orange,
Just an orange!

Artists are tuned in to thinking in colour – it is part of their life. If you look carefully at things around you, you will often notice colours and tints that you didn't know existed.

There is a story about the painter, Turner, who was well-known for his paintings of beautiful sunsets. A lady looked at one of his paintings and said, 'I have never seen all those colours in a sunset'. Turner replied, 'Ah, but don't you wish you could?'

You may have seen small 'rainbows' coming from the sloping edge of a mirror, a piece of crystal or a prism. It was not until 1666 that people understood the colours of the rainbow. In that year Sir Isaac Newton discovered that when a beam of white light passes through a glass prism it splits into its different colours.

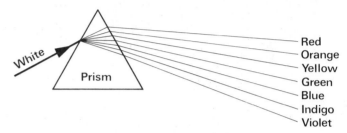

The raindrops are nature's prism. As the rays of the Sun enter a raindrop they bend. They bend again as they pass out of it.

The Sun's rays are broken up into the seven colours of the rainbow – red, orange, yellow, green, blue, indigo and violet – always in that order.

Things to do

1. Make your own rainbow: Choose a sunny day and stand with your back to the sun. Use a garden hose to make a fine spray of water, or throw a stone into a pool of water so that it makes a big splash. Look for colours in the drops of water which splash up.

Better still, try to have a look at a glass prism if you can so that you can see how the white light is broken up into colours.

2. Make your own colour chart. Divide a sheet of paper into thirty small squares. Mix together two or three of the three primary colours (blue, red and yellow) to make other colours. Here are two to start you off:

Mix yellow and blue to make green.

Mix blue and red to make purple.

If you add white to a colour you will get a different *tint* of that colour. If you add black to a colour you will get a different *shade*.

Colours of the rainbow

The piece you are going to play is about the colours you see in the rainbow. These colours are always the same, and always appear in the same order – red, orange, yellow, green, blue, indigo and violet. Although it may seem rather strange, many people say that they can 'hear' colours. They think of high notes for light colours and deep notes for dark colours.

Two composers, Rimsky-Korsakov and Scriabin, have said that different keys and scales in music suggest colours to them. For some keys and scales they each thought of the same colour – for example, they both thought that D major sounded like yellow, but for some of the other keys they thought very differently – for example, Rimsky-Korsakov felt that C major reminded him of white, but Scriabin thought of C major as red. So we can see that it was very much a matter of personal opinion and ideas. But it is strange how they both arrived at similar conclusions on a number of occasions.

Music for you to play

You will need a conductor and eight groups of players to play this piece. Each group plays sounds for one of the colours of the rainbow. If your group has one of the warmer colours such as orange or yellow, you will need a high-pitched instrument. If your group has one of the colder colours such as blue or violet, you will need a lower-pitched instrument. Each of the groups has a pattern of notes on the score which it repeats over and over again until the conductor gives the signal for everyone to stop. (This pattern of notes is rather like the *ostinato* in *The Planets* by Holst.)

THE CONDUCTOR

Give down-beats to show the beginning and end of the 10-second (10″) note for the beam of white light. You must also decide when the piece is to end and give a down-beat to tell the players to stop playing.

GROUP 1 (1 player)
Beam of white light passing through the prism
Play a pure clear sound on a recorder on the note G.

GROUP 2 Red
Use a soprano xylophone. Play with a hard felt beater.

GROUP 3 Orange
Use a soprano metallophone. Play with a hard rubber-headed beater.

GROUP 4 Yellow
Use a soprano glockenspiel. Play with a wooden-headed beater.

GROUP 5 Green
Use an alto metallophone. Play with a soft felt beater.

GROUP 6 Blue
Use an alto xylophone. Play with a medium-hard felt beater.

GROUP 7 Indigo
Use a bass metallophone. Play with a woollen-headed beater.

GROUP 8 Violet
Use a bass xylophone. Play with a felt-headed beater.

The score

The music starts with a beam of white light. This sound lasts for 10 seconds (10″). When the beam of light has passed through the prism and has split into different colours, you all start playing the sounds for your colours together, using the notes in your square on the score. Watch for the conductor's beat. It is important that you all start together. The conductor will decide how long he wants the piece to last and will give the signal for you to stop playing. Then let the sounds die away naturally.

It will help you to keep in time if you play a small accent on the first note of your pattern each time you repeat it.

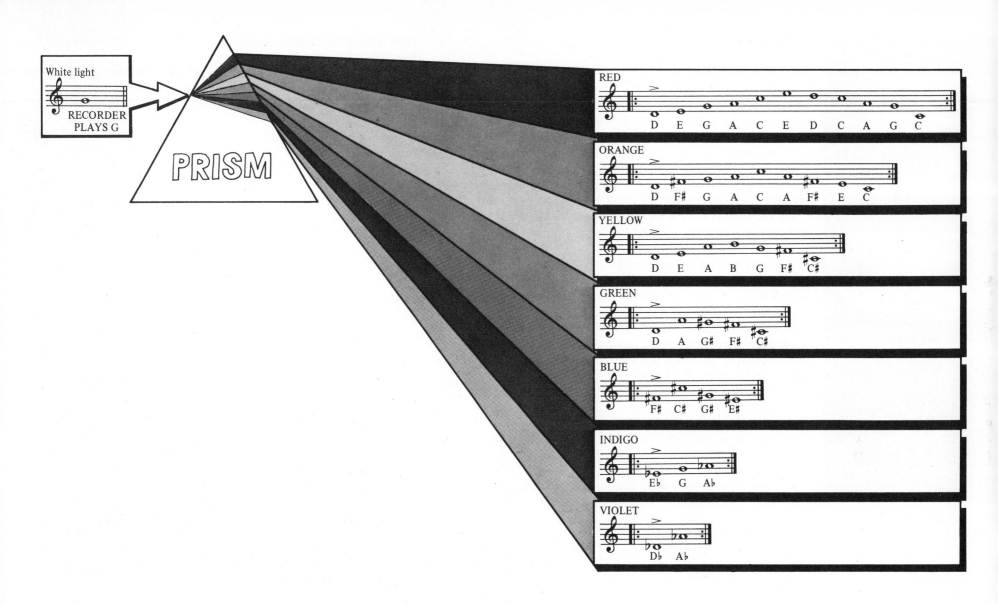

Listening

Composers often hear colour and music together.

When you next see *Top of the Pops* on television, notice how patterns and colours are often used as a background to the music. Some discos use equipment that is linked-up to the record being played. The equipment is sensitive to sound – lights flash and patterns change in time with the rhythm of the music.

Laseriums link colour and shape to music. Laser beams are projected onto a screen, and produce all sorts of wonderful shapes and colours to accompany the music being played.

But these ideas are not all new. Musicians have, for a long time, invented all sorts of weird-looking machines to combine music and colour.

A professor of art at Queen's College in London, A. Wallace Rimington, invented a Colour Organ in 1895. Music could not be played on the organ itself, but the organ projected colours on a screen to accompany piano and orchestral music by Chopin and Wagner. When trumpets blasted out a tune by Wagner, the organ flooded the screen with bright orange. When the same music was played softly by the violin, the screen changed to a pale lemon colour.

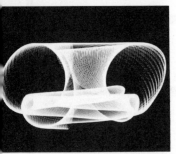

Laser patterns – from a show at the London Planetarium

A Colour Symphony

Sir Arthur Bliss, an English composer, said that when he was composing he always saw colours in his mind for the music. He was so interested in this idea of colour and music, that he composed *A Colour Symphony*. This is what he said about the symphony:

> 'While I was sketching the shape of the four movements, I came across a book dealing with heraldry, in which I read of the symbolical meanings associated with various colours: purple, red, blue, green etc. I was influenced by this, and gave each movement of the Symphony a character corresponding to a particular colour and its heraldic significance'.

Sir Arthur Bliss composed this symphony in 1922. It is written for a large orchestra, including six timpani (kettledrums) and two harps.

FIRST MOVEMENT **Purple** – the colour of Amethysts, Pageantry, Royalty and Death

This movement is played at a slow speed, suitable for ceremonial occasions such as Royal processions. There are three short sections, with a climax in the middle section. The music is very like a procession. The first, soft section, is the procession in the distance but coming towards us. The loud, middle section, is the procession passing right by where we are standing. In the final section the procession disappears into the distance.

SECOND MOVEMENT **Red** – the colour of Rubies, Wine, Revelry, Furnaces, Courage and Magic

This is a gay and light-hearted movement with glittering sounds and exciting rhythms.

THIRD MOVEMENT **Blue** – the colour of Sapphires, Deep Water, Skies, Loyalty and Melancholy

The music here is flowing and graceful. The composer wrote:

'At many places throughout is heard a rhythm of chords that I liken to the lapping of water against a moored boat, or stone pier.'

FOURTH MOVEMENT **Green** – the colour of Emeralds, Hope, Youth, Joy, Spring and Victory

This movement works up to an exciting climax to end the symphony.

Singing

There are hundreds of well-known songs about colours. Green, for example, has been thought of as the symbol of love. *Greensleeves*, *Green grow the rushes oh!* and *The Green Green Grass of Home* are just three examples.

Greensleeves is a lovely old English folk tune. Some people say that it was composed by King Henry VIII. The British composer, Vaughan Williams, liked this tune so much that he wrote a piece called *Fantasia on Greensleeves* based on it.

Here is one way to perform *Greensleeves*: Sing it through without accompaniment, then play the tune through on recorders. Go back to the beginning and sing it through once more, this time with the recorders accompanying the music.

Many songs have been written about colours. One of them, *Sing a Rainbow*, was made popular by Cilla Black.

Greensleeves

A - las my love you do me wrong to cast me off dis - court - eous - ly, And I have lo - ved you so long de - light - ing in your com - pa - ny. Green - sleeves was all my joy, Green - sleeves was my de - light; Green - sleeves was my heart of gold, and who but my la - dy Green - sleeves.

Sing a Rainbow

Red and yel - low and pink and green, Pur - ple and or - ange and blue, I can sing a rain - bow, sing a rain - bow, Sing a rain - bow too. Lis - ten with your eyes, Lis - ten with your eyes And sing ev' - ry - thing you see. You can sing a rain - bow, sing a rain - bow, sing a - long with me. Red and yel - low and pink and green, Pur - ple and or - ange and blue. Now we can sing a rain - bow, sing a rain - bow, Sing a rain - bow, too.

27

Your own compositions

We use words every day of our lives to communicate with people. Words and sentences have patterns and shapes. Speaking and singing are very similar in some languages. Chinese is a difficult language to learn because you can give the same word different meanings just by changing the pitch of your voice.

You have already discovered that some colours are warm, and others cold. The same is true of words. Some words sound soft and gentle, for example, love, warm, good, beautiful, orange. Other words are short and crisp, for example, cold, wet, black, white. Sounds like 't', 'd', and 'b' are hard, whereas 'f' 'l' and 'm' are softer sounding. There is a rhythm and a kind of tune in the sentences we speak. It is boring to listen to someone telling a story all on one level or note. If you say, 'How are you?' this 'sound-picture' could be written down as:

or, 'I don't like him', as:

To make your own 'sound-picture' you will need one group of people for each colour. Make soft and hard sounds and use the full range of your voices, from whispering to shouting. Some sounds will curl upwards, and others will droop down depending on the sort of word you are saying. Always keep in mind the feeling of the words and the rhythm of the sounds.

When you have decided on a colour for each group, recite these well-known sayings, phrases and words. Start with each group on its own, then with everyone joining in together.

Black: black sheep of the family, black hole of Calcutta, black Maria, black pudding, blackmail, blacksmith, Black Rod.
White: white collar worker, Whitehall, white horse, white elephant, white wedding, have it in black and white, white as a sheet.
Blue: blue in the face, blue ensign, blue with cold, blue blood, once in a blue moon, bluebell, bolt from the blue.
Red: Red Cross, red hot, red herring, red letter, redwood, red sky at night, red in the face.

Colour quiz

1. How good is your memory?
The colours used in road signs are black, white, red, blue, green and yellow. Copy out these signs and colour each with its correct colour.

2. The missing word in the following song titles is a colour. The colours are the same as those used for the road signs. In the bracket after each title you will find the number of the road sign which is the same colour as the one you need to complete the song title. Use this to help you only if you have difficulty finding the answer. The first title has been filled in for you.

	Colour of the road sign
a) BLUEberry Hill by Fats Domino	(3)
b) The .... bells of Scotland	(3)
c) .... is the colour of my true love's hair	(2)
d) .... Christmas by Bing Crosby	(1)
e) .... Submarine by The Beatles	(2)
f) A .... r Shade of Pale by Procol Harum	(1)
g) .... Rubber Ball by the Cyrkle	(5)
h) .... , ... Grass of Home by Tom Jones	(4)
i) .... River by Christie	(2)
j) Paint it .... by the Rolling Stones	(6)
k) Mellow .... by Donovan	(2)

ANIMALS

Cat!

Cat!

Cat!
Scat!
After her, after her,
Sleeky flatterer,
Spitfire chatterer,
Scatter her, scatter her
Off her mat!
Wuff!
Wuff!
Treat her rough!
Git her, git her,
Whiskery spitter!
Catch her, catch her,
Green-eyed scratcher!
Slathery
Slithery
Hisser,
Don't miss her!
Run till you're dithery,
Hithery
Thithery
Pfitts! pfitts!
How she spits!
Spitch! spatch!
Can't she scratch!
Scritching the bark
Of the sycamore-tree,
She's reached her ark
And's hissing at me
Pfitts! pfitts!
Wuff! wuff!
Scat,
Cat!
That's that!

– by Eleanor Farjeon

Many of you will have pets at home. Your school may well keep animals such as hamsters, rabbits or goldfish.

Some of the most popular films and television programmes are about animals. Because people are interested in animals there are many rhymes, poems, stories, pictures and songs about them. Almost every living creature has been pictured on postage stamps.

Here is a small selection from the 'stamp zoo'.

Things to do

Produce a magazine about animals on your own or with some of your friends. As there is so much you could include you will need to choose a few topics that interest you. Here are some ideas you might use:

Animal life and behaviour: zoos; wild animals; household pets; birds; animals in stories, poems, paintings, songs, films, television and comics; the circus; farm animals; prehistoric animals; insect life; fish and ocean creatures; animals in sport (such as horses, bulls and pigeons).

The giant panda – one of the threatened animals the World Wildlife Fund is trying to save

Include some or all of these features in your magazine:
a) A description of a pet of your own, or one you have known; its appearance, any funny experiences you have had with it and the way you feel about it.
b) A quiz section with questions about animals.
c) Information about rare or threatened animals and about the work of the World Wildlife Fund in trying to save them.
d) A survey of the animals owned by the rest of the class. What do they call their pets? Include a competition for unusual and interesting names for pets. (In *Old Possum's Book of Practical Cats*, the poet, T. S. Eliot gives the cats very amusing names. There is Skimbleshanks, the railway cat; Macavity, the mystery cat; Growltiger and his lady Griddlebone.)
e) A section about animals you admire or fear or find beautiful or ugly.
f) A table showing the difference in life spans of animals. (For example, the mayfly which is born at lunchtime is old by 4 pm and dead by 5 pm. Whales live so long that it is believed that there are some still alive today which were young when James I of England was king, in the 17th century.)

Ants on the move

In some hot countries like Central Africa there are species of ants which capture live creatures for food. Some of these ants are called driver ants and they are very much feared. Millions of ants hunt in long columns and together they can be as dangerous as savage tigers. Even the largest and fiercest of animals are helpless against the ants, and will be eaten alive unless they can escape to the safety of water.

Can you imagine it! Not only timid antelopes, but the powerful elephant, the rhinoceros and the frightening gorilla all crash their way through the jungle as fast as they can. They all flee from a little creature no bigger than your thumb nail – the driver ant.

Music for you to play

You will need a conductor and seven groups of players for this piece.

THE CONDUCTOR

Give a down-beat to show the beginning and end of each animal sound. The length of each sound is marked for each animal on the score to help you. (If the players are very skilful you could manage without a conductor and use a clock with a large second-hand to time the sounds for yourselves.)

GROUP 1 The driver ants

There are three different sounds for the ants:

1. Play this rhythm softly on a side-drum using your fingers or some drumsticks:

The rhythm should be even and should last for the whole piece.

2. Play sandblocks (2 or 3 people). Rub these together in the same rhythm as above.

3. Use your voices to recite these short phrases:
march along, march along, push and move along;
ants in your pants, ants in your pants;
look out! look out! here we come, here we come.

The ants march in a long line with a regular, steady rhythm. The sounds for the ants are heard on their own at the beginning of the music but they carry on right through the piece.

GROUP 2 **The gorilla** GROUP 5 **The antelope**

GROUP 3 **The elephant** GROUP 6 **The rhinoceros**

GROUP 4 **The lion** GROUP 7 **The mice**

Groups 2 to 7 should make up their own sounds for this piece. When your group plays its music it is important to describe the way the animal moves as well as imitating its sound. For example, the rhinoceros sometimes charges, the lion leaps and the antelope hops about. For animals that leap, invent some music with leaps in it.

You could imitate big, slow leaps:

or small, fast leaps:

Mice scamper and scurry around making rustling sounds. Sometimes these movements are fast, sometimes slow. Use high, quick notes played on the xylophone or rub sandblocks together. To make a scratching noise, scratch your fingernail on a drumskin. Use a large drum to make the sounds of large, plodding animals like the elephant.

Don't forget to use your voice! Remember that you can make very many different sounds with it.

Make up some words to use for your animal music – *grrr* sounds for fierce animals and slow, ponderous sounds for heavy animals.

These are only some ideas of what you might do. Think of other sounds you can use to make the sound of your group's animal. Try out some of the sounds you are going to use before you begin to play the piece of music from the score.

The score

This is really a picture of what happens. The ants' noises begin as they march along the track. As they get near to the first group of animals, the group plays its sounds. The group goes on playing until the conductor gives a down-beat for them to stop. The ants continue marching until all the animals have played their sounds. At the end of the piece all the animals panic and stampede towards the water. This is when all the groups play their sounds together for 20 seconds.

'The Carnival of Animals is a zoological fantasy'

Listening

The Carnival of Animals by Saint-Saëns

This group of short pieces by the French composer, Saint-Saëns (1835–1921), describe different members of a rather unusual musical zoo. The music is for two pianos, flute, clarinet, two violins, viola, cello and double bass. These are some of the pieces from Saint-Saëns's suite.

Royal March of the Lion

After a fanfare, the king of beasts has a royal march. He sometimes interrupts with loud roars.

Hens and Cocks

The music paints a vivid picture of cocks crowing and hens clucking, arguing and quarrelling.

The Elephant

Saint-Saëns composed some humorous music here to describe the heavy-footed elephant which sometimes swings its trunk from side to side. The elephant tune is played, as you might expect, by the largest of the string instruments – the double basses.

Personages with Long Ears

Listen to the musical impersonation of these donkeys making their *ee-aw* sound.

The Swan

The swan glides through the water. The cello plays the tune and the piano accompanies with a rippling sound for the water.

Finale

The musical zoo now reappears. See how many of the animals you can hear in this exciting end to the music.

Planet of the Apes

The music for this film was composed by Gerry Goldsmith. There are many unusual and interesting sound effects in the score.
There is the sound used at the start of the film and also when the astronauts cross the desert into the forbidden zone. This sound is made by two sorts of instruments:

1. A gong which is scraped with a triangle beater.
2. Horns blown with their mouthpieces turned upside-down.

As the astronauts see the strange, unearthly scarecrows, there are some high percussion sounds. These are made by hitting stainless steel mixing bowls. The composer also uses a ram's horn and a bass slide whistle in music that often changes speed. There are high, shrill noises, then low grunts and soft sounds.

When Charlton Heston says 'take your filthy paws off me, you dirty ape' a simple chord is all that is used. This scene is so effective that the audience usually claps and cheers at this point!

Singing

Here are two songs for you to sing about animals. The first is, *Daddy's taking us to the zoo*, a modern folk-song by the American singer, Tom Paxton.

1. Daddy's taking us to the zoo tomorrow.
   Zoo tomorrow – zoo tomorrow –
   Daddy's taking us to the zoo tomorrow.
   We can stay all day.
   Chorus

2. See the elephant with his long trunk swinging,
   Great big ears and long trunk swinging,
   Sniffing up peanuts with the long trunk swinging,
   We can stay all day.
   Chorus

3. See all the monkeys scritch, scritch scratching,
   Jumping all round and scritch, scritch scratching,
   Hanging by their long tails, scritch, scritch scratching,
   We can stay all day.
   Chorus

4. Big black bear all huff huff a-puffing,
   Coat's too heavy, he's a huff huff a-puffing,
   Don't get near the huff huff a-puffing
   Or you won't stay all day.
   Chorus

The animals went in two by two is a traditional song about the animals going into Noah's ark to survive the floods. This is a humorous song about a serious story.

1. The animals went in two by two . .
   The Elephant and the Kangaroo . .

2. The animals went in three by three . .
   The wasp, the ant and the bumble bee . .

3. The animals went in four by four . .
   The great hippopotamus stuck in the door . .

4. The animals went in five by five . .
   By eating each other they kept alive . .

5. The animals went in six by six . .
   They turned out the monkey because of his tricks . .

6. The animals went in seven by seven . .
   The little pig thought he was going to heaven . .

Daddy's taking us to the zoo

The animals went in two by two

33

Your own compositions

Make up some tunes to go with these silly rhymes by Spike Milligan. Use chime bars, glockenspiels or xylophones, and any or all of these six notes:

First tap the rhythm of the words, then invent your tune.

Sardines

A baby sardine
Saw her first submarine:
She was scared and
   watched through a peephole.
'Oh, come, come, come,'
Said the sardine's mum,
'It's only a tin full of people.'

Alligator

From Sydney Zoo
An Alligator
Was put on board
A flying freighter.
He ate the pilot
And the navigator
Then asked for more
With mashed potater.

The story of a dog and a record label

Mark Barraud was an actor born in 1847. One day he bought a dog for his children. The dog was devoted to his master, and even used to appear on stage at the theatre with him. When the actor died, his family split up and the dog was taken in by Mark's brother, Francis, who was an artist. The dog often listened for Mark, so Francis painted a picture of him with his head to one side. He added an old gramophone (called a phonogram) to the picture, and sent it to the Edison Bell Gramophone Company. He gave the picture a title – *His Master's Voice*.

The record company were not interested at first, so Francis painted another version using a more modern gramophone. This time they liked the painting and paid £100 to use the idea as their trademark.

The picture is still used today by the record company – His Master's Voice (HMV).

Animal quiz

1. Here is a list of songs about animals and birds. Use a piece of tracing paper large enough to cover the word puzzle. Then when you have found the name of the animal or bird, put a circle round its name. The word may go up and down, across, diagonally, backwards or forwards.

a) *Octopus's Garden* by the Beatles
b) *I am the Walrus* by the Beatles
c) *Tie me Kangaroo down* by Rolf Harris
d) *Tiger* by Abba
e) *Jonathan Livingston Seagull* by Neil Diamond
f) *Puff the Magic Dragon* by Peter, Paul and Mary
g) *Bluebird* by Wings
h) *There once was an Ugly Duckling* by Danny Kaye

A	D	B	L	U	E	B	I	R	D	K	L
B	F	G	H	M	R	S	W	A	L	T	E
Q	K	L	N	O	W	A	L	R	U	S	O
D	A	E	D	U	C	K	L	I	N	G	R
C	N	O	N	E	O	C	P	T	D	E	F
H	G	E	C	S	O	O	P	T	G	O	D
J	A	W	T	T	A	O	E	I	R	S	R
D	R	D	U	C	U	S	T	O	O	M	A
R	O	W	A	L	T	P	U	W	P	O	G
A	O	K	A	N	G	E	U	T	I	G	O
S	E	A	G	U	L	L	R	S	W	L	N
T	B	L	U	E	E	O	N	P	B	D	E

2. Write out the titles of these pieces of music and fill in the blank with the name of an animal, bird or insect. The anagrams (jumbled words) will give you the answer if you sort the letters out.

a) The Thieving . . . . by Rossini (*A bird* – PAMGIE)
b) . . . . Lake by Tchaikovsky (*A bird* – SNAW)
c) Flight of the . . . . by Rimsky-Korsakov (*An insect* – BLEBUM EBE)
d) The . . . . Overture by Vaughan Williams (*An insect* – SPAWS)
e) Peter and the . . . . by Prokofiev (*An animal* – FLOW)
f) Madame . . . . by Puccini (*An insect* – TUBFLERTY)

DREAMS

A Nonsense Poem

I dreamed a dream next Tuesday week,
Beneath the apple-trees;
I thought my eyes were big pork-pies,
And my nose was Stilton cheese.
The clock struck twenty minutes to six,
When a frog sat on my knee;
I asked him to lend me eighteenpence
But he borrowed a shilling from me.

Most people dream for about 100 minutes each night. We usually have between three and six dreams, and these can last as little as 10 minutes or as much as 30 minutes each. The dreams just before waking are longer than the earlier ones. Everyone dreams, but some people never remember dreaming. Others remember only a little of the dream they had just before waking up. No-one remembers every dream.

Dreams are imaginary pictures, but they are often about what happened to us the day before. Some dreams are pleasant and some are frightening. The frightening ones are called nightmares.

Artists, writers and musicians have sometimes had 'creative dreams'. The writer, Samuel Taylor Coleridge, in a sleep of 3 hours, dreamed over 200 lines of poetry. When he woke up, he quickly started to write down the lines. Unfortunately, someone interrupted him after he had written only ten lines and he forgot the rest. But he did finish the poem, *The Rime of the Ancient Mariner*, from some of the ideas in his dream.

Many people remember having had very interesting dreams. Perhaps you have dreamed about trains, bridges, rivers, roads, kings and queens or small animals. These are thought by some people to have particular meanings, or to be symbols for other ideas.

Kings and queens are thought to mean your parents and small animals mean children. Crossing a bridge or a river can stand for a turning point in your life. A house is thought to be the body or mind and the rooms of the house are different parts of the body.

Some objects that you dream about may be the result of the way you feel at the time or of something in the room where you are sleeping. A dry throat may make you dream about the desert or a buzzing fly might become a dive-bomber.

A pun is a word which sounds like another word but has a different meaning. Word puns often happen in dreams. Scientists have conducted experiments with people to see if puns come up in their dreams. On one occasion some people were shown two pictures just before they went to sleep.

Many of the people dreamed about a uniformed officer – a Captain in the Navy or Army. They had combined Cap and Ten to make Captain.

**10
TEN**

Things to do

Keep a dream notebook. Write down what you remember about your dreams in it. You may well find that some dreams crop up over and over again. When you have kept a diary and written down your dreams for a time, try to work out what they mean:

a) Look for symbols in your dreams. What were the things that you dreamt about and what do they mean?
b) Look for puns in your dreams and make a list of them in your notebook.

Nightmare

The piece you are going to play is a musical picture of a rather frightening dream. It begins when a clock chimes six times. An alarm clock can be heard ticking right through the piece. At first the person hears sounds around him such as the weather outside. The person slowly sinks into dreamy sleep. During the next 60 seconds his dream begins.

After 2 minutes, the dreamer wakes briefly and hears his heart beating. He goes straight back to sleep and to his dream. Something starts to chase him and he runs away in a panic, slowly at first, then as fast as he can. His heart beats faster. Then there is about 5 seconds of silence as his dream ends. The alarm clock rings and he wakes up!

Music for you to play

You will need a conductor and eleven groups of players for this piece. For the silent sections in the piece you will have to watch the conductor very carefully so that everyone begins and ends neatly together.

THE CONDUCTOR
Give a down-beat every 15 seconds (15″). You will also need to give the players a very clear sign for the beginning and end of the silences.

GROUP 1 (1 player) **The striking clock**
Play six separate beats on a tubular bell or gong, using a soft beater.

GROUP 2 (1 player) **The ticking clock and the alarm bell**
The ticking clock begins at the beginning of the piece and carries on right through to the end. Place the clock on the table in the middle of the other players. Wind up the alarm bell, pull out the alarm button and turn the hands of the clock to a time about 5 minutes before the alarm bell is set to ring. At the end of the piece, be ready to turn the hands round to the right time to make the alarm bell ring. You will need to be ready for this if you are to make the alarm bell sound at just the right time.

GROUP 3 **Clear and muffled sounds as the person goes to sleep**
There are three sounds for this group to play:

1. Play any selection of high notes on a glockenspiel using a metal beater but from time to time run the beater up and down the bars.
2. Use a suspended cymbal and rub a violin or cello bow across the edge of it.
3. Play muffled sounds on chime bars. To do this, first hit the bar in the normal way, then pass a strip of cardboard backwards and forwards over the hole in the wooden tube.

Dream sounds (Groups 4 to 9)

GROUP 4
Put some small beads, or something similar, into a metal wastepaper bin. Roll the beads around in the bin slowly and gently, then more quickly.

GROUP 5
Put carpet tacks into a tambourine. Swirl them round slowly.

GROUP 6
Use descant and treble recorders to play soft, slurred, 'eery' notes.

GROUP 7 (2 or 3 players)
Hit triangles with metal beaters.

GROUP 8
Use a coconut shell cut in half, and rub the two pieces together.

GROUP 9
Use plastic frozen food bags and crumple them to make your sounds.

GROUP 10 **The dreamer's heartbeat**
Use a wobble board to make the sounds for the dreamer's heart beating.

GROUP 11 **Footsteps**
There are two sounds for this group:

1. Hit the wooden part inside a xylophone box with hard beaters.
2. Use castanets for the part of the dream where the dreamer starts to run more quickly.

GROUP 1

GROUP 2

GROUP 3

GROUP 4

GROUP 5

GROUP 6

GROUP 7

GROUP 8

GROUP 9

GROUP 10

GROUP 11

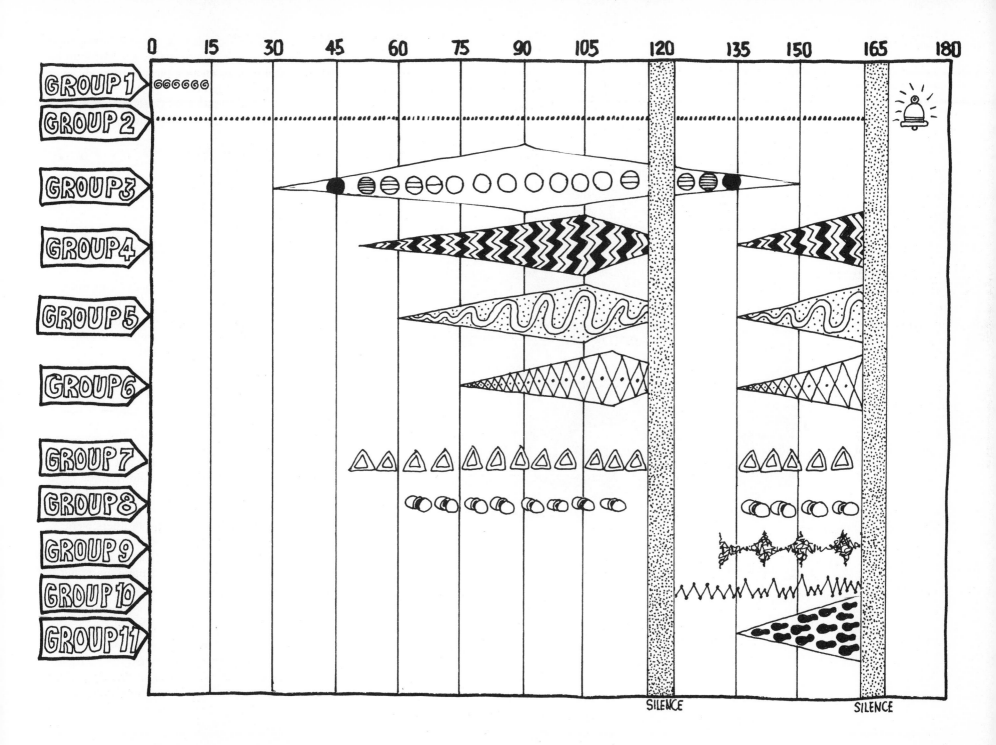

SILENCE

SILENCE

Listening

The strange dream

Tartini, the famous violinist and composer, was born in Italy in 1692. His great interests in life were music and fencing. When he was twenty, Tartini married one of his pupils in secret. His wife was related to the powerful Cardinal of Padua, who did not agree with this marriage to a mere musician. The Cardinal ordered Tartini's arrest, so Tartini had to escape dressed as a monk. He decided to hide away in a Monastery where he could study music in peace.

One night after going to bed in his monk's cell, Tartini had a strange dream. The Devil appeared in this dream and offered to grant any of his wishes. One of Tartini's requests was that the Devil should play his violin. The music was so good that Tartini woke up in amazement. He quickly began to write down this marvellous music, but alas, he started to forget the tunes. Tartini himself finished the music, which he thought was the best he had ever written. The music has since become known as *The Devil's Trill* sonata.

A trill is a musical shake between two different notes.

It is written: [musical notation] and played: [musical notation]

Sonata is an Italian word for 'sounded' or 'played'. It was used to describe instrumental music, whereas *cantata* was music to be sung. But *sonata* is mostly used to mean a piece in several movements for one or two instruments.

The music of *The Devil's Trill* sonata is in three movements. The first movement begins with a slow and flowing tune:

The second movement is lively and robust, and uses some of the lowest notes of the violin:

The last movement has many changes of mood – sometimes slow, sometimes fast. Near the end there are many trills with *double stopping*. (This is a special effect where the violinist plays on two strings at once so that two notes can be sounded together.) The trills begin low down, and rise, note by note:

Joseph and the amazing technicolour dreamcoat

This is a 'pop' musical composed by Tim Rice and Andrew Lloyd Webber. It is about the Old Testament story of Joseph and his multi-coloured coat.

Joseph was his father's favourite son and his brothers were jealous of him. He dreamed that he was the most important member of the family. Later, when he was in Egypt, his dreams came true. Joseph became the Pharoah's right hand man after he had explained the meaning of the Pharoah's dreams.

THE MUSIC

The music for *Joseph* has all sorts of interesting and exciting things in it. There is a choir of young voices accompanied by several instruments, including a pop group. When the Pharaoh tells of his dreams, he sings a rock 'n roll song in the style of Elvis Presley. The choir is a backing group and they sing *Bop-shu-wah-doo-wah*. Joseph was first performed in a school. It was so popular that it was later staged in a West End theatre in London.

Singing

Here are two short songs about dreams for you to sing.

1. *Jacob's Ladder* is a traditional English song from the 19th century. The Old Testament part of the Bible has many dreams recorded in it. Apart from Joseph's dreams, perhaps the most famous one is Jacob's dream of the ladder reaching up to heaven. The story comes in the first book of the Bible (Genesis).

When you have sung *Jacob's Ladder* through a few times, sing it as a round with two groups of singers (**A** and **B**).

The first group (**A**) starts to sing at the beginning of the melody. The second group (**B**) starts to sing from the beginning of the melody when group **A** reaches letter **B** on the music. When each group reaches the end of the melody the singers should go back to the beginning and start again.

2. *I dreamed a dream* is a nonsense song, but dreams can often be a strange mixture of things!

As well as *Joseph and the amazing technicolour dreamcoat*, Tim Rice and Andrew Lloyd Webber have composed other hit musicals. *Jesus Christ Superstar* and *Evita* have been seen by millions of people all over the world. Although these other two musicals call for professional performers to play and sing the music, there is no reason why your class or school could not perform *Joseph*. It was written for a school, and is great fun to sing and play, so you could perform it at your school.

Jacob's Ladder

1. As Jacob with travel was weary one day, At
2. This ladder is long it is strong and well-made, Has stood

night on a stone for a pillow he lay, He
hundreds of years and is not yet decayed;

cresc.

saw in a vision a ladder so high, That its
millions have climbed it and reached Zion's hill,

dim.

foot was on earth, and it's top in the sky.
thousands by faith are climbing it still.

I dreamed a dream

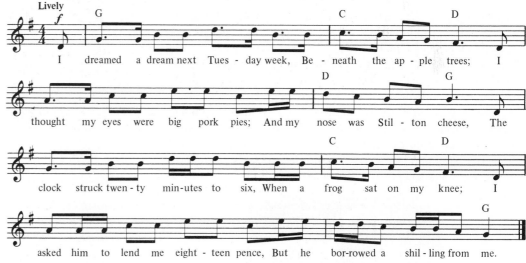

I dreamed a dream next Tuesday week, Beneath the apple trees; I

thought my eyes were big pork pies; And my nose was Stilton cheese, The

clock struck twenty minutes to six, When a frog sat on my knee; I

asked him to lend me eighteen pence, But he borrowed a shilling from me.

Joseph is given the multi-coloured coat by his father, Jacob

Your own compositions

One of the ways composers find ideas for music is to think of the instruments they will use. There is a lot of noise in the world today, and many composers are thinking of smaller and more interesting sounds to use in their music.

1. For a piece about a quiet and peaceful dream, think of soft and gentle sounds to use. You could, for example, use a musical mobile. It can be made from small pieces of glass or metal, ping-pong balls, lengths of bamboo cane or pieces of tinfoil. It will make a tinkling sound as the pieces bump into each other.

The zither is another instrument that can make delicate and interesting sounds. Slither boxes, a lagerphone and a bottle organ would also be useful in this type of music.

Use these ideas and think of other simple, quiet and interesting sounds for your own music. One of the advantages of playing a quiet piece of music is that people listening will have to sit up, take notice and concentrate more on the music.

2. As a contrast, perhaps you would like to make up a piece of music about a very different kind of dream. It is a dream about witches who appear on dark and windy nights.

Imagine that the wind is howling through the trees in a wood. It is raining; dark shadows move in the bushes and you hear evil laughter. Flashes of lightning and the rumble of thunder bring the witches to life. They dance around, chanting spells and laughing. Then the cock crows and they quickly disappear into the forest.

For a piece of music on this theme you could use instruments like maracas, sandblocks, slither boxes and cymbals for the wind and rain. You could use voice sounds for the wailing cat noises, laughing, cackling and evil spells. Imitate the thunder with a large drum. Build up the music to a loud climax. When the cock crows, the wind and rain carry on for a few seconds, then all the sounds stop together.

Dream quiz

1. You have been dreaming about these objects, but each of the pictures suggests the name of a piece of fruit. Name the fruits.

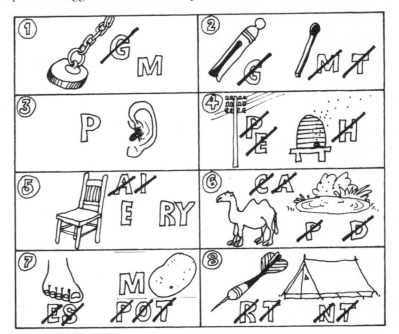

2. These are titles of music about dreams. You have to work out the name of the composer or singer.
Find this out by using the code 1 = A, 2 = B, 3 = C etc.

a) *The Sleeping Beauty* by 20. 3. 8. 1. 9. 11. 15. 22. 19. 11. 25
   A famous ballet written in 1888 by a Russian composer.

b) *A Midsummer Night's Dream* by 13. 5. 14. 4. 5. 12. 19. 19. 15. 8. 14
   Incidental music to Shakespeare's play. Composed when this German composer was only seventeen years old.

c) *Träumerei* (German for 'dreaming') by 19. 3. 8. 21. 13. 1. 14. 14
   A short, dreamy piano piece from a collection called *Album for the young* by a German composer.

d) *Imagine* by 10. 15. 8. 14. / 12. 5. 14. 14. 15. 14
   Many singers have recorded this lovely pop song, but the best-known version is the one by the composer.

e) *Last night I had the strangest dream* by 2. 15. 2. / 4. 25. 12. 1. 14
   An important folk-rock performer. He composes and sings his own songs.

Steam Locomotives

The first railways were opened more than 150 years ago. They changed the way many people lived by making travel faster than ever before. Goods of all kinds including fresh foods could now be delivered to places quite far away. Railways were the fastest and cheapest way to travel, and were soon built throughout the country. Even before the death of Stephenson (inventor of the famous Rocket engine), the steam engine had changed the life of Britain.

Locomotives were powered by steam for more than 100 years. Steam engines were iron giants that belched smoke, steam and sparks and made a thunderous noise. But they were more exciting than the efficient engines of today. Steam engines have now almost disappeared from the railways of the world, although they are still used in India, South America and parts of Spain. Some people were sad to see the old steam trains disappear and have grouped together to preserve them in working condition. Perhaps you have been on one of these private steam railways such as the Bluebell Line in Sussex or the Severn Valley Railway.

Things to do

1. Write to your nearest railway station and ask the stationmaster if you can visit his station with some of your friends to see how everything works. He may show you inside a signal box and explain how the train timetable is planned to help the trains run smoothly. When you visit the station take a notebook and cassette recorder with you. On your visit:

a) Draw a plan of the station and mark on it the platforms, buffet, waiting rooms, ticket office, magazine stall and any other things you see.

b) Make a cassette recording of the different sounds you hear such as announcements of trains arriving and departing, the guard's whistle, carriage doors slamming and express trains which rush right through the station without stopping.

2. If you live near a railway or transport museum, go to see some of the famous old steam engines. (You can often buy pictures and postcards of different engines, carriages and waggons at the museums.)

The Song the Train Sang – by Neil Adams

Now
When the
Steam hisses;
Now
When the
Coupling clashes;
Now
When the
Wind rushes
Comes the slow but sudden swaying,
Every truck and carriage trying
For a smooth and better rhythm,
For a smooth and singing rhythm.
This . . . is . . . the . . . one . . . .
That . . . is . . . the . . . one . . . .
This is the one,
That is the one,
This is the one, that is the one,
This is the one, that is the one, . . .
Over the river, past the mill,
Through the tunnel under the hill;
Round the corner, past the wall
Through the woods where the trees grow tall.
Then in sight of the Town by the river,
Brake by the crossing where the white leaves quiver.
Slow as the streets of the town slide past
And windows stare at the jerking of the coaches
Coming into the station approaches.
Stop at the front.
Stop at the front.
Stop . . . at the front.
Stop . . . at the . . . .
Stop.
AHHHHH!

Railway signals

Perhaps you have heard bells ringing as the train you are on passes a signal box. These bells are a way of sending messages along the railway line. The bell system was first used by the South Eastern Railway in 1851, and it is still used today.

This is how it works: The railway line is divided into sections. Each section has a signal box at either end. Only one train is allowed into a section at a time. This is called the 'block system'. The different bell codes are used by the signalmen to pass on information about what kind of train is approaching and whether the line is clear.

Music for you to play

Before you start the piece, try to listen to some train sounds. Then try out different groups of instruments and voices to get the best train noises. Practise clapping out the rhythm pattern a train makes on the rails. Start with a slow rhythm, then gradually build up to a much faster pattern. Use your voices to make sounds like:

clickety-click, clickety-click, clackety-clack, clackety-clack;
oo-oo for the whistle;
hisssss and *ahhhhh* for the steam.

Some useful instruments are maracas, drums, woodblocks, claves and sandblocks. You can use a mouth organ for the engine whistle. Practise: an even rhythm at 30mph, 80mph and 100mph; starting slowly then gradually getting faster.

Dynamics (louds and softs) are important. Imagine that the listener is halfway along the railway line watching the trains go by. As each train approaches its sound will get louder. As it passes by and travels into the distance the sounds will die away.

You will need a conductor and six groups of players for this piece.

THE CONDUCTOR
Give a down-beat for the bell code, then for the signal. You must also give a down-beat for each of the numbered track sections. Each track section lasts for 1 second.

GROUP 1

GROUP 1 (1 player) **The bell codes**
Use an electric or battery-operated doorbell. Sleigh bells would be a good alternative. The bell codes you will be using are on the opposite page.

GROUP 2 **Signals**
Red (danger). Play a group of notes on xylophones.
Green (clear). Play a group of notes on glockenspiels.
   If you sound the red signal to stop the train, you must sound the green signal after 5 seconds to start the train again.

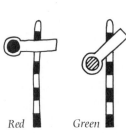
Red   *Green*
GROUP 2

GROUP 3 **Express passenger train**
Play an even and fast rhythm of 100mph.

GROUP 4 **Branch passenger train**
Gradually build up speed to 50mph.

GROUP 5 **Express freight train**
A noisy train. Play an even and fast rhythm of 80mph.

GROUP 6 **Light engine**
Gradually build up speed to 30mph. Use lighter sounds for this engine.

Players in Groups 3, 4, 5 and 6 (trains) will find their bell codes on the opposite page.

Order of playing

1. (Group 1) Sound the bell code for the type of train. (The bell code player will decide on which train this is to be.)
2. (Group 2) Sound the signal – red or green. If you make the sound for red you must sound green 5 seconds later.
3. (Groups 3, 4, 5 or 6) The train passes through the section.
4. (Group 1) Sound the bell code to show that the train is out of the section (all clear). The bell code can then be sounded for the next train to start its journey through the section. Repeat the same order for each train.

GROUP 3

GROUP 2

GROUP 1

GROUP 4

| 1 | 2 | 3 | 4 | 5 | 6 | 7 | 8 | 9 | 10 | 11 | 12 | 13 | 14 | 15 | 16 | 17 | 18 | 19 | 20 |

GROUP 5

GROUP 6

TYPES OF TRAIN INTO SECTION	BELL CODES
Express passenger (3)	🔔 🔔 🔔 🔔
Branch passenger (4)	🔔 ░ 🔔 🔔 🔔
Express freight (5)	🔔 ░ 🔔 🔔 ░ 🔔 🔔
Light engine (6)	🔔 🔔 ░ 🔔 🔔 🔔
Trains (all types) out of section	🔔 🔔 ░ 🔔

 Bell ringing ░ Silence

43

Listening

Pacific 231 by Arthur Honegger

Honegger was born in 1892 at Le Havre in France. He was fascinated by trains and used to watch them for hours as a boy.

'I have always had a passion for locomotives. To me they are living beings . . .'

The music is written for a large orchestra. The composer's description of the music is probably the best one:

'In Pacific 231 I have not aimed to imitate the noise of an engine, but rather to express in terms of music a visual impression and physical enjoyment. The piece opens with the quiet breathing of the engine at rest, the straining at starting, the gradually increasing speed. Three hundred tons of weight, thundering through the silence of the night at a mile a minute.'

'The subject of my composition was an engine of the 'Pacific' type number 231, used for heavy loads and built for great speed.'

The music is, however, also a picture of the locomotive itself. Despite what Honegger says, we hear all the sounds of this iron monster. It was one of the earliest pieces of music written about the machine age.

Listen to the exciting sounds and notice how, as the music gets slower, more and more notes are heard.

The Little Train of the Caipira by Villa-Lobos (1887–1959)

Villa-Lobos is the best-known Brazilian composer. He wrote a large number of different works and was very interested in his country's folk music.

This piece describes a journey made by a small mountain train in Brazil. You can hear it start, build up speed, stop at a station, pull off again, and then stop with a lot of fuss and steam.

The orchestra includes a saxophone and some rather unusual Brazilian percussion instruments, such as maracas and a guiro. (A guiro is a large gourd, and is played by scraping a stick across notches cut into its surface.)

A guiro

This is the tune played by the violins as the train clatters along on its journey:

Murder on the Orient Express

This is an exciting film about a famous steam train – the Orient Express. It is based on the thriller by the well-known writer, Agatha Christie. It is about a group of people who travel on the train and are suspected of murder. The action of the film is set on the train itself.

An English composer called Richard Rodney Bennett composed the music. He uses some clever sounds and rhythms to represent the train. As the Orient Express starts its marathon journey, we hear the hiss of escaping steam and the engine's whistle. You can feel the tremendous power as the train leaves the station and builds up speed.

Singing

Casey Jones

The chorus has parts for maracas and a side drum (played with wire brushes). Use two recorders for the train's whistle.

2. Put in your water and shovel in your coal,
   Put your head out the window,
   Watch the drivers roll,
   'I'll run her till she leaves the rail
   'Cause we're eight hours late with the Western Mail'.
   He looked at his watch and his watch was slow,
   Looked at the water and the water was low,
   Turned to his fireboy, then he said,
   'We're bound to reach 'Frisco
   But we'll all be dead.'
   Chorus

3. Casey pulled up Reno Hill,
   Tooted at the crossing
   With an awful shrill.
   'Snakes all knew by the engine's moans
   That the hogger at the throttle was Casey Jones.
   He pulled up short two miles from the place,
   Freight train stared him right in the face,
   Turned to his fireboy, 'Son, you'd better jump
   'Cause there's two locomotives
   That are going to bump.'
   Chorus

4. Casey said just before he died
   'There's two more roads
   I'd like to ride.'
   Fireboy asked, 'What can they be?'
   'The Rio Grande and the Santa Fe.'
   Mrs Jones sat on her bed a sigh'n,
   Had a pink that her Casey was dy'n,
   Said, 'Hush you children, stop your cry'n,
   'Cause you'll get another Papa
   On the Salt Lake Line.'
   Chorus

Rounders: slang for drifters and loafers
Hogger: a dirty person
Caller: a person who wakes other people up early in the morning

45

Your own compositions

With the sounds and information you have collected on your visit to a railway station, build up a sound atmosphere piece about a railway station. Include all the bustle, activity and noise.

You could use ideas such as the announcements of arrivals and departures, the guard's whistle, the train hooting and carriage doors slamming. With the right sounds and some imagination, you could make an interesting and vivid picture for your listeners.

If you cannot record the effects live, try imitating the sounds with your voices and instruments, or use sounds from a sound effects record as part of your piece. (There are lots of records available with sounds of trains on them.)

It may help to imagine that your sound picture is to be used for the opening scenes of a film, which are being shot in a station. Decide on the mood you are trying to create. Pick out the details as well as the general feeling, just as Honegger does in *Pacific 231* and Richard Rodney Bennett does in his music for the *Orient Express*.

One of London's railway stations – Liverpool Street

Railway quiz

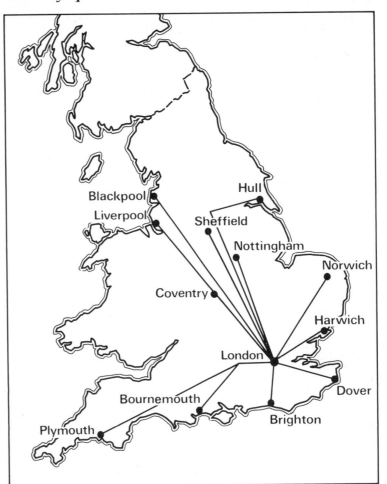

On the map you will find some of the railway lines to towns and cities. You have to match up the place names on the map with the following clues.

a) The Beatles and a famous football team come from . . . . .
b) Robin Hood and the Sheriff of . . . . .
c) Lady Godiva rode through the streets of . . . . . on horseback, but not past the magnificent new Cathedral there
d) Three seaside resorts beginning with B
e) Two famous ports or docks
f) . . . . . is famous for its steel used to make knives, forks and spoons

MACHINES

A machine is a man-made device that makes work easier to do. Try to open a tin of food without a tin-opener. It is very difficult to do. A tin-opener is a simple machine, but you need it to do this simple job. The tin-opener will only work with your help. You have to provide the power or force to make the parts move.

Engines and motors were invented and factories were built and became filled with large machines that could work for 24 hours each day. Tractors and lorries are used for many of the jobs that farm animals used to do. Sailing ships were replaced by large steam ships. The motor car replaced the horse and cart and now people use it to travel hundreds of miles.

Many machines are based on quite simple ideas. One of the oldest ideas is that of the wheel and axle. You will be able to think of many machines where this is used. If you look at a wheelbarrow, for example, you will be looking at something which has changed very little since it was first invented. If you look at the number of ways the wheel and axle idea is used in a car, you will see that the basic idea has developed a long way.

Some of the machines which you may find inside and outside your home

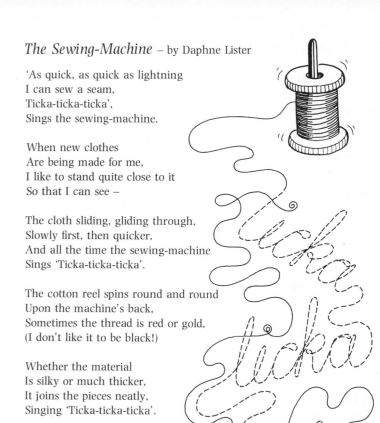

The Sewing-Machine – by Daphne Lister

'As quick, as quick as lightning
I can sew a seam,
Ticka-ticka-ticka',
Sings the sewing-machine.

When new clothes
Are being made for me,
I like to stand quite close to it
So that I can see –

The cloth sliding, gliding through,
Slowly first, then quicker,
And all the time the sewing-machine
Sings 'Ticka-ticka-ticka'.

The cotton reel spins round and round
Upon the machine's back,
Sometimes the thread is red or gold,
(I don't like it to be black!)

Whether the material
Is silky or much thicker,
It joins the pieces neatly,
Singing 'Ticka-ticka-ticka'.

'Watch the seams grow quickly,
The neatest ever seen,
Ticka-ticka-ticka',
Sings the sewing-machine.

Things to do

1. Choose one or two machines inside your home (e.g. vacuum cleaner, washing machine) and one or two outside (e.g. lawn-mower, bicycle) and have a look at them. Explain how the job they do would have been done before they were invented and say how the machine you have chosen makes the job easier.

You could also try to find out how the machine works and whether it is simple or complicated.

2. Make a recording of some machine sounds. Choose machines that you often hear, such as electric mixers or vacuum cleaners. Have a competition with your friends to see if they can identify the machine sounds.

47

A car journey

The music you are going to play is about a car journey from your home to school. During the journey you will meet several things that will cause you to slow down, stop, indicate, turn corners and so on.

Music for you to play

To play this piece you will need a conductor and eight groups of players.

THE CONDUCTOR

Decide how long each incident lasts, and also how much time there is between each of the incidents. You will also act as the policeman at the zebra crossing (incident 9). Decide when to start and stop the traffic and give the signs.

GROUP 1 **The car engine sounds**

This is the largest group, and could have as many as ten players. Many engines have a sequence of sounds which change as the engine gains speed. As you journey round the route you will travel at different speeds, but whatever the speed you should try to keep the rhythm of the engine steady and even. When you have to stop at traffic lights, a road junction or crossing, the engine sounds should carry on but be quite slow and quiet.

Try different instruments such as maracas, castanets, claves, sandblocks, comb and tissue paper, drums and voice sounds (*chsssh, mmmm, vroom*) and choose the ones you think make the best engine sounds.

When you have chosen your instruments, practise starting the engine (have a few false starts), revving up the engine, speeding up (play louder as the speed gets faster) and steady speeds at 30mph, 40mph and 70mph.

GROUP 2 (two players) **The car's indicators**

Play two different high notes on xylophones with hard beaters. Each player plays one of the notes.

GROUP 3 **Push-button pedestrian crossing**

As the car approaches the crossing, the green man is showing, so the car will have to stop. When the red man shows, the car can move ahead.
Green man – two players make a high, bleeping sound for 10 seconds, using chime bars or voice sounds.
Red man – after 10 seconds two other players each hit a cymbal with a soft-headed stick. Let the sound carry on until it dies away.

GROUP 4 (one player) **The car's horn**

Use an old-fashioned rubber bulb horn to make a good sound. If you are not able to use one of these, think of another instrument or use your voice!

GROUP 5 **Traffic lights**

Use tubular bells or large glockenspiels for these. When the conductor gives the signs, play a low note for *red*, followed by a low note and medium note together for *red and amber*, then a high note on its own for *green*. (There should be a gap of about 2 seconds between each light change.)

GROUP 6 (one player) **Police car overtaking**

Use a trumpet or cornet to play the two notes for the car horn. The sound starts softly in the distance and gets louder as the car overtakes.

GROUP 7 **Windscreen wipers** (two-speed)

Use your voices to make sounds like *swisshh swisshh*. These sounds should get faster as the rain becomes harder.

GROUP 8 **Zebra crossing**

Look for the policeman's (conductor's) sign. He will probably stop the car at the crossing. Use a small drum to play repeated sounds for the flashing amber light.

GROUP 1

GROUP 2

GROUP 3

GROUP 4

GROUP 3

GROUP 4

GROUP 5

GROUP 6

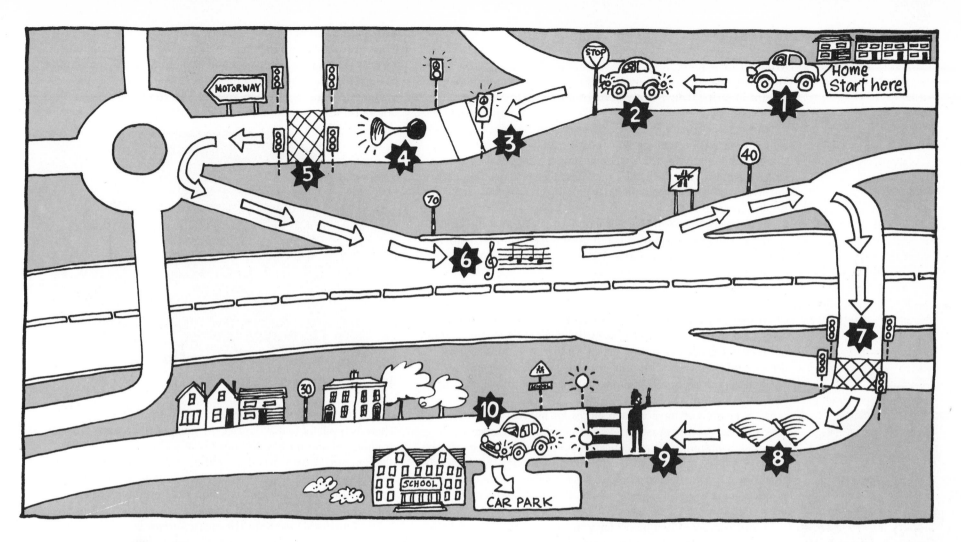

 The score

Here are the incidents of the journey, with the groups which play them.

1. (Group 1) Start and rev up the car at home and drive off.
(Group 1 plays all through the journey, but at various speeds.)
2. (Group 2) Indicate left, stop at the main road, then turn left.
3. (Group 3) Drive on and arrive at the pedestrian crossing. The green man is showing for pedestrians to cross, so the car has to stop. When the red man shows the car can drive on.
4. (Group 4) Continue on along the road. A pedestrian steps carelessly into the road. Sound the horn!

5. (Group 5) Arrive at the traffic lights. They show red so the car must stop. Then red and amber show together, followed by green so the car can drive on.
6. (Group 6) Drive round the roundabout and go onto the motorway. A police car overtakes, sounding its two-tone horn.
7. (Group 5) Leave the motorway and arrive at traffic lights.
8. (Group 7) The rain starts. Switch on the windscreen wipers.
9. (Group 8) Arrive at a zebra crossing. The car may be stopped by the policeman.
10. (Group 2) Immediately after the crossing, indicate left and turn into the school car park.

Listening

Musical boxes

Musical boxes come in many shapes and sizes and can still be bought in shops today. Many of them are made in Switzerland and exported all over the world.

You will find modern musical jewellery boxes, wine decanters, cigarette boxes and lighters. Much larger musical boxes can sometimes be found at the seaside in amusement arcades. After you have put a coin in the slot machine, figures move and dance to the music. This music is made in much the same way as in the smaller musical boxes.

A clockwork motor turns the metal barrel with the pins in it. As the pins come round they catch on the teeth of the comb. The teeth are different lengths (short teeth for high notes, long teeth for low notes).

Musical clocks

There are musical clocks that can play tunes. They work on the same principle as the musical boxes. In some of them, the sounds are made by hammers hitting bells. In others there is a small organ, and the barrel with pins works levers which open and close the organ pipes. Air is blown into the pipes by bellows, to make the musical sounds.

Many composers have written pieces for musical clocks. Haydn was an 18th century Austrian composer who wrote over a hundred symphonies, thirty concertos and eighty string quartets. But it is not so well known that he composed thirty-two pieces for clocks of this sort. Recordings have been made of some of these pieces being played on musical clocks. Some of the pieces are often played on the piano now.

Mozart composed two pieces for a machine of this kind, which was sometimes known as a *flute-clock*. These pieces are called *fantasias* and are often played in organ recitals today.

Here are two tunes from the *Fantasia in F Minor* (K.608) by Mozart:

A musical clock, showing the metal barrel with pins, the hammers and the bells

Fairground Organs

The fairground organ belongs to an age before gramophone records were invented. It was one of the only ways that ordinary people could hear popular tunes. There is a society for preserving fairground organs, so when you next go to the fair, look out for one of these wonderful pieces of machinery.

An old fairground organ

How a fairground organ works

There is a pile of folded card at the back of the organ. This card is gradually taken up into the machinery. The card has rows of different-sized holes. It is the position and size of these holes which tell the organ which notes to play and how long each note will last. (A short hole will make a short note and a long hole a long note).

The Toreador's Song from the opera *Carmen* by the French composer, Georges Bizet, is often played on fairground organs. This is how the card would be punched out with holes to make this well-known tune:

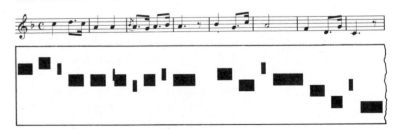

Singing

William Brown is a well-known folk song about a time when there was poverty in Britain. There were not enough jobs to go round. Even though he worked hard at his machine in the factory, William was put out of work because the factory just could not sell enough goods. In the mill towns of Lancashire, and the mining towns of Durham, there were often more people on the dole than there were at work.

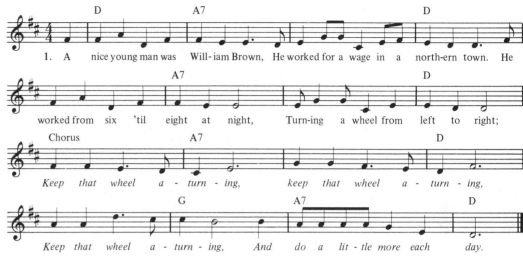

William Brown

1. A nice young man was Will-iam Brown, He worked for a wage in a north-ern town. He worked from six 'til eight at night, Turn-ing a wheel from left to right;

Chorus
Keep that wheel a-turn-ing, keep that wheel a-turn-ing,
Keep that wheel a-turn-ing, And do a lit-tle more each day.

2. The boss one day to William came,
   He said, 'Look here, young what's yer name.
   We're not content with what you do,
   So turn a little harder or it's out with you!'
   Chorus

3. So William turned and he made her run
   Three times round in place of one.
   He turned so hard he soon was made
   The Lord High Turner of the trade.
   Chorus

4. But sad the sequel is to tell,
   He turned out more than the boss could sell.
   The market slumped and the price went down,
   Seven more days and they sacked young Brown.
   Chorus

51

Your own compositions

Make up your own music about a factory. The factory is full of different types of machinery. Everyone there is busy. Men are hammering metal, welding and cutting and some are shouting. The music you compose should be loud, with lots of whirring, knocking, throbbing, banging and vibrating sounds.

Use instruments and sounds that you think will be suitable, but all the sounds must be made with metal. Metal bars, oil drums, tin trays, saucepan lids, metal dustbin lids, alarm clocks, motors, bunches of keys, gongs, and triangles could all be useful. Use your voices for shouting, whistling and singing. Factories are noisy places, so try to get a continuous sound with different noises going on. Machine noises should always be even and steady.

See how many words you can make from the word, 'machinery'. Use the words as voice sounds in your music.

The Metronome

In 1814, a German inventor called Maelzel, wanted to help musicians to decide the speed of a piece of music more accurately, so he invented the Metronome.

This mechanical instrument ticks away at a steady speed. The speed can be changed by sliding a weight up or down the arm. The numbers on the scale tell you how many ticks there are to a minute. You will often see at the start of a piece of music, a note and a figure, for example: ♩=60. This means that you set the metronome to 60, and then on each tick you play a crotchet's worth of music.

It is best to stop the metronome before you begin to play, otherwise your music could become too mechanical.

Machine quiz

1. Use the code 1 = A, 2 = B, 3 = C etc. to name the titles of these films. Each of the films is about some sort of machine.

a) 20. 8. 5. / 18. 1. 9. 12. 23. 1. 25. / 3. 8. 9. 12. 4. 18. 5. 14
   A film based on the story by E. Nesbitt, where three children prevented a train crash.

b) 2. 21. 12. 12. 9. 20
   Steve McQueen was the star of this film. He did his own stunt driving in one of the most exciting car chases ever filmed.

c) 20. 8. 5. / 20. 9. 13. 5. / 13. 1. 3. 8. 9. 14. 5
   The famous author, H. G. Wells, wrote science fiction stories. This film is based on one of his books.

d) 2. 21. 7. 19. 25. / 13. 1. 12. 15. 14. 5
   All the characters were played by children in this film. They used cream-firing machine guns called 'splurge guns'.

2. Fairground organ cards have holes cut in them to make the musical sounds. The short holes make short notes, the long holes make long notes. As the holes get higher or lower, so do the notes.

Name these three tunes:

a) Although not a pop song, this tune is probably heard more than any number one in the top twenty

b) A song from *The Sound of Music*

c) One of the Beatles' most famous songs about an underwater machine

LONDON

> 'When a man is tired of London he is tired of life; for there is in London all that life can afford'.
> *Dr. Johnson*

London is the capital city of the United Kingdom. It is one of the largest cities in the world.

The oldest and smallest part of London is the City of London, which is just one square mile in size. Surrounding the City are the London Boroughs, and together they make up Greater London. Greater London covers an area of 616 square miles.

The River Thames is one of the main reasons for London's existence. When the Romans came to Britain 2,000 years ago, they settled on the banks of the river. The river was narrow enough for bridges to be built across it, but also deep enough for large sea-going ships. Many of the important places in London, the Houses of Parliament, the Tower of London and some famous markets and palaces were built near the river.

At the centre of present-day London is Trafalgar Square with Nelson's column. If you look in the same direction as Nelson you will see Whitehall (leading to Westminster Abbey, the Houses of Parliament and the River Thames). Look to your left and you will see the Strand (leading to the City of London). If you look to your right you will see the Mall (leading to Buckingham Palace), and turning even further to the right, there is the West End with its famous shops.

Things to do

Produce a magazine on your own or with some of your friends, about London or another big city that you have visited. Britain's famous capital city is so full of sights to see and things to do that it is difficult to know where to start. The best way is to choose a few topics that interest you and go on from there. Here are some ideas that you might use:

London's history; present-day London (Post Office Tower, Stock Exchange, shops etc.); London's parks, markets and railway stations; customs and ceremonies (Changing of the Guard, Ceremony of the keys etc.); sport (Wembley, the Oval, Lord's and Twickenham); entertainment in London; cockneys (rhyming slang and pearly kings and queens).

When you have decided on the topics to include in your magazine, it will be a good idea to start to collect some information. Some useful items to have are a map of London and a plan of the Underground. Most libraries and bookshops will have a good selection of books about London. Look for pamphlets, postcards, newspaper cuttings, stamps and matchbox labels. You should bear in mind whether the magazine is for Londoners or for visitors to London.

Include some of these features in your magazine:

a) An account of a visit to London, mentioning some of the sights you saw. Include photographs and drawings.
b) A quiz with a prize for the highest number of correct answers.
c) A simple outline map of the centre of London and a list of places in that area. Ask your readers to mark the places of interest in the correct positions on the map.

This is the key of the Kingdom

This is the key of the Kingdom
In that kingdom is a city
In that city is a town,
In that town there is a street,
In that street there winds a lane,
In that lane there is a yard,
In that yard there is a house,
In that house there waits a room,
In that room there is a bed,
On that bed there is a basket,
A basket full of flowers.

River Thames journey

The piece you are going to play is about a journey down the River Thames. Your river journey gives a grandstand view of London, both past and present. It starts at Westminster Bridge and ends at the Prospect of Whitby pub. On the way you are going to see some of the most attractive stretches of this famous river.

Music for you to play

Although this is a short musical voyage, it is packed with things to play. You will need to look carefully through the incidents of the journey and follow their order on the score. You will need a conductor and nine groups of players for this piece, but there are some parts of the journey where most of you play together to make crowd noises.

CROWD SOUNDS

a) *Sounds of people walking.* Rub a nailbrush over a newspaper in short, sharp strokes.

b) *London street cries.* Shout these and any others you know:

You will need to watch the conductor to see when it is time for you to play.

THE CONDUCTOR

Give a down-beat to show the beginning and end of each incident.

GROUP 1 **Big Ben's chimes and St. Paul's bells**

For Big Ben's chimes play these notes slowly on glockenspiels:

For St. Paul's bells go on playing this scale on glockenspiels or tubular bells until you are given the signal to stop:

GROUP 2 **The boat's engine**

This sound is played throughout the piece. Use slither boxes, maracas and sandblocks and play them all using a circular movement.

GROUP 3 **Ripples in the water**

This sound is heard throughout the piece. Play chime bars and make a wavering sound by moving a piece of card backwards and forwards across the sound hole.

GROUP 4 **The orchestra rehearsing**

Use as many instruments as possible. The oboe (or another instrument) plays the note A, then all join in playing any notes, sliding up and down scales.

GROUP 5 **Cleopatra's Needle**

For this tall column, use different-sized cymbals or gongs. Play the largest one (lowest-sounding one) first, then build up one sound on top of another until you have used all the different sizes of instrument.

GROUP 6 **Passing under bridges**

Play soft rolls on a large cymbal to make the sound for the shadows.

GROUP 7 **The cold and icy Antarctic**

Make sounds for the whistling wind by using recorder mouthpieces and by making *whissssh* and *pheeeew* sounds with your voices.

GROUP 8 **Seagulls shrieking**

Wet a wine bottle cork and rub this sharply on the side of a bottle.

GROUP 9 **The execution, cannon-fire and tanker's hooter**

Execution – tap an even, slow beat on the side-drum.
Cannon-fire – play notes on a large drum with a soft beater.
Hooter – use a trombone or another large brass instrument, and play the lowest note you can. Make the note last for 5 seconds.

GROUP 1

GROUP 2

GROUP 3

GROUP 4

GROUP 5

GROUP 6

GROUP 7

GROUP 8

GROUP 9

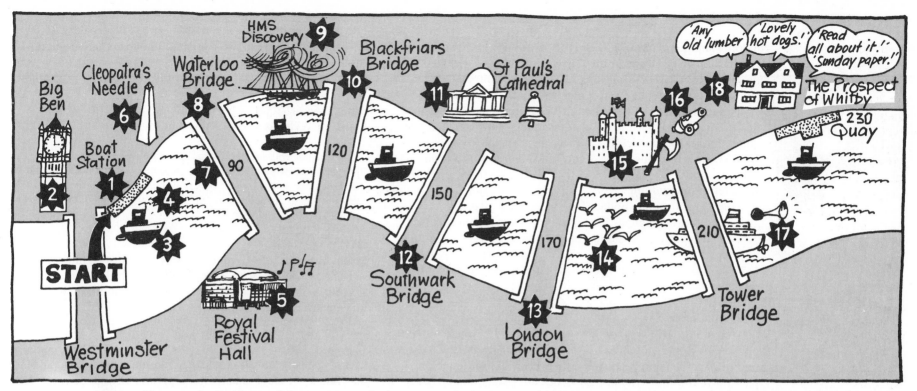

 Here are the incidents of the journey with the groups which play them. (Groups 2 and 3 will play throughout the journey, starting from the time when the boat sets off.)

1. (Everyone plays) The boat is due to leave at 3 o'clock. People are still crowding onto the water-bus, chattering excitedly.

2. (Group 1) Big Ben chimes 3 o'clock.

3. (Group 2) The boat is ready to leave now and the crew cast off. The engine throbs and vibrates and the boat chugs along.

4. (Group 3) As you leave Westminster Bridge, the boat makes small ripples in the water.

5. (Group 4) You pass the Royal Festival Hall at a steady speed and hear an orchestra rehearsing for a concert.

6. (Group 5) You pass Cleopatra's Needle (a tall granite column) on your left. It was made in Egypt over 3,500 years ago and was given to Britain in 1918.

7. (Group 6) You pass under Waterloo Bridge.

8. (Everyone plays the crowd sounds, except Groups 2 and 3) You hear the muffled roar of traffic and the sound of people's feet.

9. (Group 7) You pass the HMS Discovery, the famous ship which took Captain Scott on his voyage to the Antarctic in 1901.

10. (Group 6) The boat passes under Blackfriars Bridge.

11. (Group 1) The bells of St. Paul's Cathedral are ringing loudly across the water.

12. (Group 6) You pass under Southwark Bridge and all is quiet except for the boat's engine and the ripples in the water.

13. (Group 6) The boat passes under London Bridge.

14. (Group 8) A flock of seagulls is following the boat, making loud, shrieking noises.

15. (Group 9) To your left is the Tower of London where royalty and nobles were sometimes imprisoned, and even executed.

16. (Group 9) As the water-bus comes to the majestic Tower Bridge, you hear the sound of cannon-fire. This is sometimes used to salute special occasions such as the Queen's birthday.

17. (Group 9) Tower Bridge is about to be raised to let a large tanker pass into the busy Pool of London. The tanker sounds its loud hooter as it passes by.

18. (Everyone plays) Your journey ends at the famous old smugglers' pub – the Prospect of Whitby. You can hear cockney street-traders, newspaper vendors, fishmongers and a rag-and-bone merchant calling out their street cries.

Listening

Ralph Vaughan Williams (1872–1958) was born in Down Ampney, a small village in the Cotswolds. He spent a great deal of time in his early years travelling around the countryside to collect folksongs. Many of these songs had been passed on from generation to generation. Although Vaughan Williams was born in the country, he lived in London for much of his life. So it was quite natural that he decided to compose a symphony about London. He wrote this in 1913 and called it *A London Symphony*.

A London Symphony

A symphony is usually quite a long work, and *A London Symphony* is no exception. When you are listening to the music, pick out a small section rather than trying to concentrate on a lot at a time.

This is the plan for the symphony – it is in four movements or sections.

FIRST MOVEMENT

London sleeps. The Thames flows serenely through the city. The city begins to stir and, in the composer's own words, 'the noise and hurry of London begins'. We then hear different musical pictures of the city – Hampstead Heath on a Bank holiday, the parks and churches.

The music starts rather mysteriously, and if you listen carefully, you will hear a hint of the chimes of Big Ben. The flowing of the Thames is suggested by the strings murmuring their music. Then horns, trumpets and trombones play as the city begins to wake.

Vaughan Williams uses a number of short tunes for the bustle of the people going about their business. Here is an impatient taxi driver:

and some sailors singing a shanty:

and a cockney whistling:

SECOND MOVEMENT

The composer describes this movement as 'Bloomsbury Square on a November afternoon'. It is a damp and foggy picture at dusk. An old street musician plays *Sweet Lavender* (a London song), and the sound of a hansom cab is heard as the evening gets darker.

THIRD MOVEMENT

Vaughan Williams wrote of this movement:

'If the hearer will imagine himself standing on Westminster Embankment at night, surrounded by the distant sounds of the Strand, with its great hotels on one side, and the New Cut on the other, with its crowded streets and flaring lights, it may serve as a mood in which to listen to this movement.'

FOURTH MOVEMENT

This is rather a solemn movement. It is a musical picture of the sad side of London, with its unemployed and unfortunate people. The music ends with the chimes of Big Ben and the Thames flowing strongly but silently.

My Fair Lady

One of the best known of all stage musicals about London is *My Fair Lady*. The story is based on a play by George Bernard Shaw called *Pygmalion*. The music was composed by Frederick Loewe. The stage play was so successful that it was made into a film starring Rex Harrison, Audrey Hepburn and Stanley Holloway.

The story begins outside London's Covent Garden market in 1912, where Eliza Doolittle, a cockney girl, is selling flowers. Professor Henry Higgins is an expert in dialects, and can say where a person comes from just by hearing them speak. He has a bet that he can change Eliza's speech so that people will think that she is a duchess.

After many difficulties in her speech lessons, Eliza loses her cockney accent and sings *The rain in Spain stays mainly in the plain*. The professor puts Eliza to the test by taking her to Ascot races and to the embassy ball. Eliza passes with flying colours – some people are convinced that she is a foreign princess.

Eliza is very happy at first, and sings *I could have danced all night*. But then she wonders what is to become of her. Professor Higgins suggests that she will have to find a gentleman to marry. A refined young man called Freddy Eynsford-Hill, proposes to Eliza, and the professor is really rather sad. He cannot get Eliza out of his mind, and sings *I've grown accustomed to her face*.

Singing

In the past there were some cockney Londoners who were very fond of *ding-dongs* (sing-songs) and who often met to sing on a Saturday night in someone's front room. Sometimes they would wear paper hats, funny noses and glasses.

Some of the cockney songs are very amusing. Adults and children alike would join in the *ding-dong* which might include well-known songs like *Maybe it's because I'm a Londoner, Chase me Charley, I do like to be beside the seaside, I've got a lovely bunch of coconuts* and the *Hokey Cokey*.

Here is a less well-known cockney song, *They're moving father's grave*, for you to sing.

A scene from the film version of 'My Fair Lady'

They're moving father's grave

Oh, they're mov-ing fath-er's grave to build a sew-er, They're mov-ing it re-gard-less of ex-pense. They're shift-ing his re-mains, to put in five inch drains, To ir-ri-gate some posh bloke's res-i-dence. Now in his life-time fath-er nev-er was a quit-ter, And I'm sure that he won't be a quit-ter now, For when that job's com-plete, He'll haunt that priv-vy seat, And he'll on-ly let them sit when he'll al-low. Oh, won't there be some aw-ful con-ster-na-tion, And won't those ci-ty chap-pies rant and rave, Which is no more than they de-serve, To have the bare-faced nerve, to muck a-bout with a Brit-ish work-man's grave.

57

Your own compositions

In the City of London there are many tall buildings. Here is an idea for making an interesting piece of music by using the shape of part of London's skyline as a score for your music. In *River Thames journey* (Page 54) you used the idea of sounds being built on top of each other to represent a tall column (Cleopatra's needle). In the music you are going to compose now, you can show the different heights of London's skyscraper buildings. Different sounds should be used for the different materials of the buildings (steel, glass and concrete).

Imagine that this drawing is part of the skyline:

Glass & Steel   Concrete   Glass, steel & Concrete

You will need to use instruments which give you a good choice of size and pitch. For example, you will need instruments with bright and shiny sounds for a building made of steel and glass. Cymbals, triangles, glockenspiels and chime bars all come in different sizes. If you decided to use cymbals, you would need several sizes ranging from large, 30 cm (12 inch) ones to small, 10 cm (4 inch) ones.

Start by striking a 30 cm (12 inch) cymbal, then a 25 cm (10 inch) one and gradually work through the sizes to the 10 cm (4 inch) one, building the sounds on top of each other as you strike each new cymbal. In this way your music will give an idea of the height of the building and it will be the right sound for steel.

Choose one of the other instruments to make your sounds for the glass parts of the building. When you have tried out all the steel and glass sounds and decided what to use, play all the sounds together.

A concrete building will need much duller sounds. The wooden bars on a xylophone would be a good choice. Build the sounds up again as you did with the steel and glass sounds.

If you are trying to show a wide building in your music, wait longer before playing the next sound. If you want to suggest that it is a narrow building, play the sounds closer together.

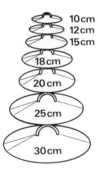

10 cm
12 cm
15 cm
18 cm
20 cm
25 cm
30 cm

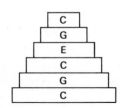

C
G
E
C
G
C

London quiz

Have you ever said 'let's have a butcher's' when you want to look at something? If you have, did you know that you were using cockney rhyming slang? A true cockney is a person born within hearing distance of Bow bells (near Fleet Street). Cockneys have a language of their own. It is called rhyming slang. Here is an example:

I was sitting in front of the *Jeremiah* (fire)
A-warming me *plates of meat* (feet)
When there comes a knock at the *Rory O'More* (door)
That made me *jam tart* (heart) beat.

Make up some sentences or poems of your own by using the rhyming slang below. See if your friends can work out what you are saying.

Parts of the body
Alive or dead (head); *bacon and eggs* (legs); *bread and cheese* (knees); *north and south* (mouth); *plates of meat* (feet); *Hampstead Heath* (teeth).

Relations
Trouble and strife (wife); *sorry and sad* (dad); *skin and blister* (sister); *hot cross bun* (son); *bottle of water* (daughter); *baker's dozen* (cousin).

Clothes
Whistle and flute (suit); *canoes* (shoes); *pair of kippers* (slippers); *round the houses* (trousers); *tit-for-tat* (hat); *fourth of July* (tie).

Instruments

There are many sections of this book where you will be playing music which needs lots of different instruments. You will already have some of the instruments you need in the classroom, but you will also need to make some of your own instruments to create interesting sounds. Some are quite simple to make and can be made from everyday bits and pieces.

You can experiment with different instruments to see how many different sounds you can get. How many different sounds do you think can be made from one chime bar? Here are some that you could try:

1. Hit the chime bar with different kinds of beaters.
2. Rub the chime bar with a metal beater or a nail.
3. Move a piece of card backwards and forwards over the soundhole. This will open and close the hole, making a wavering sound.

Some of the instruments you may have in the classroom

Classroom instruments

Skin instruments
These include side drums, bass drums, tom-toms, timpani (kettledrums), bongos, tambours and tambourines.

Wood instruments
These include xylophones (different sizes), castanets, woodblocks, claves and maracas.

Metal instruments
These include glockenspiels (different sizes), chime bars, tubular bells, tuning forks, cymbals (different sizes), gongs (different sizes), triangles (different sizes), sleigh bells, Indian bells and metallophones (different sizes).

Keyboard instruments
These include pianos and electronic organs.

More unusual instruments
These include flowerpot bells, glass jars and bottles (with or without water), bunches of keys, metal trays, saucepan lids, alarm clocks, motors, electric bells, comb and tissue paper, nailbrushes and scrubbing brushes with newspaper, wine glasses, wine bottle corks, sandblocks, wobble board, coconut shells and rattles.

Voices
Your voice is one of the most useful instruments you are likely to find – it can make all sorts of sounds and noises.

Tape recorders and cassette recorders
Sounds are often more interesting when they are recorded and played back at different speeds. Here are some hints on making a recording:
1. Have the microphone at the right distance from the players so that everyone is heard.
2. Watch the recording level and get it just right. Too low is as bad as too high.
3. Make sure that you have enough tape left on the spool. Recordings are often spoilt when the tape runs out just before the end of the piece.
4. Be careful not to press the stop button until the last note has died away completely.

Instruments to make

Sandblocks

WHAT YOU NEED
1. Two pieces of wood about 120mm by 100mm – roughly postcard size
2. Two cotton reels
3. Sandpaper
4. Glue, nails or screws

HOW TO MAKE
1. Sandpaper the two pieces of wood to make them smooth.
2. Stick, screw or nail the cotton reels onto the middle of the backs of the wood. Make sure that the screws or nails do not come through to the front of the wood.
3. Cut the sandpaper to the size of the flat pieces of wood and stick it down onto the wood.

HOW TO PLAY
1. For a continuous sound, rub the two blocks together in a circular motion.
2. To make a rhythmical sound, rub the blocks backwards and forwards.
3. Clap the blocks together before rubbing them.

Claves

WHAT YOU NEED
Two pieces of dowel rod about 150mm long (about the length of a pencil)

HOW TO MAKE
Sandpaper the ends to make them smooth.

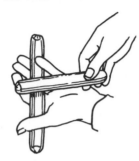

HOW TO PLAY
Hold one of the claves in your hand, and tap the claves together.

The sound will change if you hold the claves tightly, or if you tap them in different places. You could make several different pairs of claves using different thicknesses of dowel rod. Each pair would then make a different sound.

Coconut shells

WHAT YOU NEED
A coconut

HOW TO MAKE
1. Saw the coconut in half.
2. Remove the contents.
3. Sandpaper the inside and outside down to the hard shell.

HOW TO PLAY
Hit the coconut shells together. See how many different sounds you can make with them. (Coconut shells make a crisp, hollow sound and are good for imitating the sound of horses' hooves.)

Wobble board

WHAT YOU NEED
A large sheet of hardboard measuring about 100cm by 50cm

HOW TO PLAY
1. Hold the shorter edges, one in each hand, and bend the board backwards and forwards.
2. Hold the board by one of the shorter edges and shake it. (This makes unusual sounds and can sometimes sound like thunder.)

Slither boxes

WHAT YOU NEED
1. A metal box or biscuit tin
2. Beads, dried peas, small pebbles or bird seed (These will all make different sounds, so make several slither boxes and use different fillings in each)
3. Adhesive tape

HOW TO MAKE
1. Put the filling into the tin. (Be careful not to put too much in.)
2. Seal the edges of the tin with adhesive tape.

HOW TO PLAY
1. Hold the tin in both hands and tip it slowly from side to side.
2. Use fast movements from side to side. (This will make good steam engine sounds.)
3. Use a circular movement to make a continuous sound.
4. Move the tin very gently. (This will make sounds like the sea lapping gently onto a pebble beach.)

Zither

WHAT YOU NEED

1. Two pieces of wood, one 30cm by 18cm, the other 18cm by 4cm
2. Ten L-shaped screw hooks
3. Five large, strong rubber bands or five lengths of piano wire

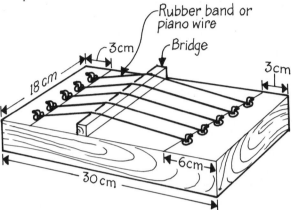

HOW TO MAKE

1. Take the larger piece of wood with the longer sides facing you.
2. Measure in 3cm from the left-hand end of the wood and draw a pencil guideline.
3. Measure in 3cm at the top of the right-hand end, and 6cm at the bottom of the right-hand end and join the marks you have made with a diagonal pencil guideline.
4. Measure out 5 equal 3cm divisions along each of the guidelines, and screw in the L-shaped screw hooks.
5. Stretch rubber bands across opposite hooks, or twist lengths of piano wire around opposite hooks to make them firm. (You will need pliers for tightening the wire.)
6. Slide the smaller piece of wood (the bridge) under the rubber bands or wires so that they rest on it.

HOW TO PLAY

Pluck the strings with your fingers. You can alter the pitch of the notes by moving the bridge up and down.

Lagerphone (or jingles)

WHAT YOU NEED

1. Forty metal bottle tops
2. One long nail
3. Two pieces of wire, each about 50cm long
4. One strong metal staple
5. One length of broom handle about 70cm long
6. Some adhesive tape
7. A pair of pliers

HOW TO MAKE

1. Remove the plastic or cork discs from inside the bottle tops. (You may find this easier if you soak the tops in hot water first.)
2. Punch a hole in the middle of each top, using the nail.
3. Put one piece of wire on top of the other to make a cross shape. Then twist the two wires together where they cross.
4. Staple the twisted part firmly onto one end of the broom handle.

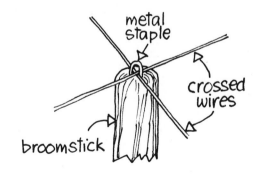

5. Thread ten bottle tops onto each of the four ends of wire.

6. Bend each of these wires down to make a semicircle.
7. Fasten the loose ends of the wires firmly to the handle using adhesive tape.
8. Wind a short piece of wire over the tape to fasten it firmly to the handle.
9. Use the pliers to twist the wire tight. Snap off the loose ends.
10. Cover the wire with more adhesive tape.

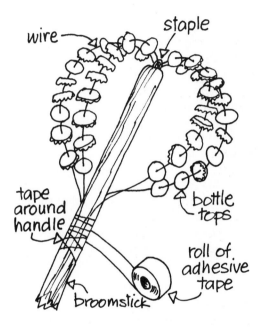

HOW TO PLAY

1. Hold the lagerphone in your hand and shake it using firm wrist movements.
2. Strike the bottom of the broom handle on the floor.

Flower pot bells

WHAT YOU NEED
1. A number of different-sized clay pots (You can usually find these at a garden centre)
2. Strong wire (Allow about 50cm for each pot you make)
3. Short pieces of bamboo cane or dowel rod
4. A broom handle

HOW TO MAKE
1. Tap the pots and listen to the sounds. Choose enough different sounds to make up a scale or part of a scale. Arrange the pots in order of size – large, low-sounding pots to small, high-sounding ones
2. Take a length of wire (about 50cm) and bend it into a U-shape. Then cross the ends over to make a loop that is slightly larger than the broom handle. (The size of the loop is important as you are going to hang your flower pot bell on the broom handle to play it.)
3. Hold the loop you have made in your left hand, and twist the two wires round and round each other, leaving about 10cm untwisted at the ends.
4. Take a short piece of cane and make a loop round it. Then continue twisting the wires together until you reach the ends.

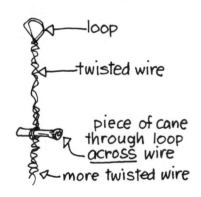

5. Slide the piece of cane out of the wire loop.
6. Push the ends of the wire down through the hole in the bottom of a medium-sized flower pot, making sure that the loop for the piece of cane goes inside the pot.

7. Open out the loop you made for the piece of cane and push the cane back into the loop. Tighten the wires inside the pot with pliers. (The piece of cane will stop the wires coming back through the hole in the pot.)

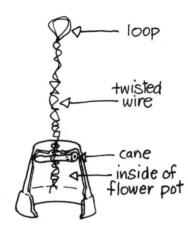

8. Hang the flower pot bell from the broom handle using the first loop you made. (The broom handle can be supported on two chairs.)
9. When you have made a medium-sized flower pot bell you can go on to make some larger and smaller ones as well. Use shorter lengths of wire for the large pots and longer lengths for the smaller ones. When you hang them up, all the rims of the bells will be at the same level and this will make them easier to play.

pots large to small

HOW TO PLAY
Use a soft-headed beater and hit the pots on the rims.

Bottle bells

WHAT YOU NEED
Instant coffee jars (You will need two small, two medium and two large ones)

HOW TO MAKE
Add a little water at a time to each of the jars and test the sound by tapping them lightly. Use the larger jars for low notes and the smaller ones for high notes. Make a complete scale or part of a scale.

HOW TO PLAY
Hit the jars gently with a beater.

Bottle organ

WHAT YOU NEED
1. One large instant coffee jar.
2. A plastic or cardboard tube. (You can use a kitchen towel roll centre but you will need to wrap some adhesive tape round the bottom half of the roll to prevent it from becoming soggy.)

HOW TO MAKE
1. Half-fill the jar with water.
2. Lower the tube down through the neck of the jar into the water.

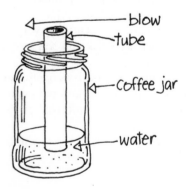

HOW TO PLAY
Blow across the top of the tube as you move the tube up and down in the water to make different notes.

Musical mobile

WHAT YOU NEED

1. A length of thick galvanised wire about 80cm long
2. Some adhesive tape
3. A long nail
4. Ping-pong balls, short lengths of bamboo cane or small pieces of tinfoil
5. A reel of cotton
6. Three lengths of chain or strong string

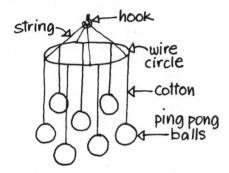

HOW TO MAKE

1. Bend the galvanised wire to form a ring. (You could use a large biscuit tin or sweet tin to help you get a good shape.)
2. Twist the two ends of the wire together and cover the join with adhesive tape.
3. Carefully make a hole in the ping-pong balls, bamboo cane or tinfoil, using the nail.
4. Thread a length of cotton about 40cm long through each of the holes and make a secure knot to hold the cotton in place.
5. Tie the other end of the cotton onto the wire ring.
6. Fasten the three pieces of string or chain to the wire circle.
7. Hang your mobile from a hook in the ceiling.

HOW TO PLAY

1. Blow gently on the mobile.
2. Hang it near to a door when there is a draught. (The mobile makes a gentle tinkling sound as the pieces bump into each other.)

Some easy-to-make beaters

WHAT YOU NEED

1. For all these beaters you will need materials to make various types of head. Some of them are hard and others are soft.
2. All the beaters need some sort of handle. This can be made from dowel rods, bamboo cane or even more unusual things such as empty ballpoint pen barrels.

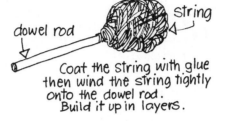

Coat the string with glue then wind the string tightly onto the dowel rod. Build it up in layers.

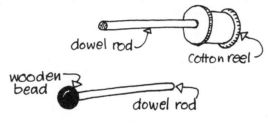

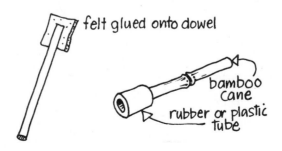

Maracas

WHAT YOU NEED

1. Two empty washing-liquid containers.
2. Two lengths of dowel rod about 20cm long to fit the neck of the bottle.
3. Rice, dried peas, gravel or small nails.
4. Adhesive tape.

HOW TO MAKE

1. Remove the stopper from each bottle.
2. Put a handful of the rice or other filling into each bottle.
3. Fit a dowel rod into each bottle, leaving enough for you to hold comfortably. Wrap adhesive tape round the top of each bottle to hold the dowel rod in place.
4. Decorate the maracas by painting them and adding colourful designs. Make several pairs of maracas using different fillings in each to make different sounds.

HOW TO PLAY

1. Hold the maracas upright and move your wrists firmly backwards and forwards.
2. To make different sounds, hold the maracas horizontally, and use other movements of your wrist such as circular movements.

Guitar chords

C

G

F

D

A

E

D7

A7

Am

LONGMAN GROUP LIMITED
Longman House
Burnt Mill, Harlow, Essex CM20 2JE, England

First published 1982
ISBN 0 582 20001 6

*Set in 10/12 Photina 747, Monophoto
by Servis Filmsetting Limited, Manchester*

*Printed in Hong Kong by
Wing Tai Cheung Printing Co Ltd*

Acknowledgements

We are grateful to the following for permission to reproduce copyright material:

The author, Neil Adams for his poem 'The Song The Train Sang' from *Travelling Light*, published by Oliver & Boyd; The author, Stanley Cook for his poem 'Snowing' from *Come Along* by Stanley Cook, Dept. of English Studies, Huddersfield Polytechnic; Faber Music Ltd. on behalf of J. Curwen & Sons, and Boosey and Hawkes (Canada) Ltd. for an extract from 'Mars' from *The Planets* by Gustav Holst © 1949 by J. Curwen & Sons Ltd.; Dobson Books Ltd. for the poems 'Sardines' and 'Alligator' from *A Book of Milliganimals* by Spike Milligan; EMI Music Publishing Ltd. for an extract from 'Presto' from *Four Sketches For Today* by Paul Sturman, © 1977 by EMI Music Publishing Ltd.; Essex Music International Ltd. for the song 'Going To The Zoo' by Tom Paxton, published by Harmony Music Ltd.; Author's agent for the poem 'Cats' by Eleanor Farjeon from *The Children's Bells*, published by Oxford University Press; William Heinemann Ltd. for the poem 'The Sea' from *The Wandering Moon* by James Reeves, published by William Heinemann Ltd.; the author, Daphne Lister for her poem 'The Sewing-Machine' © Daphne Lister; Chappell Music Ltd. for an extract from the song 'Sing A Rainbow', words and music by Arthur Hamilton from *Pete Kelly's Blues* © 1955 Mark VII Music, British publisher Chappell Morris Ltd.; G. Ricordi & Co. for an extract from 'Little Train' by H. Villa-Lobos © G. Ricordi & Co. Reproduced by arrangement; Stainer & Bell Ltd. for an extract from 'London Symphony' by R. Vaughan Williams.

We are grateful to the following for permission to reproduce photographs: Aerofilms, page 53; BBC Copyright, page 8 right; BBC Hulton Picture Library, pages 32 left and 56; Bentley and Humphrey, *Snow Crystals*, McGraw Hill Book Company, page 18 right; Biblioteca de Bologna, page 3 below; Bibliothèque Nationale, Paris, page 2; Columbia-EMI-Warner, page 10; EMI Music Archives, page 34; Keystone Press Agency, page 26 right; Laserium at the London Planetarium, page 26 left; Mansell Collection, pages 8 left and 15; Mary Evans Picture Library, page 38; Museo Civico Bibliografico Musicale, Bologna, page 20; Newberry Library, Chicago, page 3 above; Maurice Nimmo, page 23; Playhouse, Harlow, page 39 (photo Len Toms); Paul Price-Smith, page 11; Ann Ronan Picture Library, page 51; Royal Greenwich Observatory, page 6; Space Frontiers/AG Astrofotografie, page 5; Studio 49, Munich, page 59; John Topham Picture Library, pages 18 left, 35 and 50 right; Twentieth Century Fox, pages 32 right and 57; Universal Pictures/CIC, page 14 right; Victoria and Albert Museum, pages 27 and 50 left; H.R. Viollet, pages 14 left (Collection Viollet), 44 above left (Albin-Guillot-Viollet) and 44 below left (Boyer-Viollet); World Wildlife Fund, page 29 right.

Longman Photo Library, pages 46, 47 and 52.